Welcome to New York

1

T0163896

One World Trade Center
© DelensMode/Moment RM/Getty Images

Getting to New York

FROM JOHN F. KENNEDY (JFK)

jfkairport.com
24 km/15mi southwest of Manhattan.

Shuttle – go to Ground Transportation. $20-25 per person and 1hr-1hr30min.

Taxi – 40-90min depending on traffic. Set price for Manhattan $52, 80 cent surcharge, $4.50 rush hour surcharge, plus tip ($1-2).

Car services – Lyft, Via, and Uber all pick up at JFK. Prices vary depending on whether you share a car or take a private ride. Expect to pay minimum $30 to Manhattan.

NY Airport Service – Links to (every 20-30min), Penn Station, Port Authority and Grand Central. At Grand Central, there are shuttles for guests staying in hotels located between 23rd and 63rd Sts. $18. 1hr-1hr30min. www.nycairporter.com

Subway – Take the **AirTrain** to the subway. Depending on your destination, take the **A**, **J**, or **E** lines. Expect 60min on subway. Faster is taking the **LIRR** (regional train) to either **Penn Station** (if your destination is in Manhattan) or **Atlantic Terminal** (if in Brooklyn). AirTrain: $7.75 plus $2.75 for the subway; LIRR: $7.75.

Getting around by public transport

Bus and subway run daily 24hrs - $2.75/single ticket. **Pay-Per-Ride MetroCard** *– Top up at any subway station. New card $1. You can swipe up to four times in a row.* **7-Day Unlimited Ride MetroCard** *(7 days) – Unlimited journeys - $33 - can only be swiped every 18 min.*

FROM LAGUARDIA (LGA)

laguardiaairport.com
13 km/8mi east of the city center.
Shuttle – Follow signs for Ground Transportation. Expect $20 per person and 30-45min.
Taxi – Expect $35-55 for Manhattan, plus tip and around 30min.
Car services and NY Airport Service – Same as JFK.

FROM NEWARK (EWR)

newarkairport.com
26 km/16mi southeast of Manhattan, in New Jersey.

Taxi – Expect $40-70, plus tip and surcharge of $5 at rush hour, and 45min-1hr.
Train – The **AirTrain** links to the trains connecting Newark to New York (Penn Station). Combined AirTrain + NJ Transit ticket: $15.25.
Car services – Same as JFK.

Grand Central Terminal
© spyarm/iStock

3

Unmissable

Our picks for must-see sites

Greenwich Village★★
Map A-B6 - ♿ p. 40

Museum of Modern Art★★★
Map C4 - ♿ p. 58

Central Park★★★
Map D3, C-D4, E2 -
♿ p. 67

**Metropolitan Museum
of Art★★★**
Map D3 - ♿ p. 74

**One World
Observatory★★★**
Map A8 - ♿ p. 18

Empire State Building★★★
Map C5 - ♿ p. 54

Brooklyn Bridge★★★
Map B8 - ♿ p. 26

Soho★★
Map B7 - ♿ p. 32

Times Square★★
Map C5 - ♿ p. 53

Statue of Liberty★★★
Map A8 - ♿ p. 22

5

Our top picks

💚 **Sip a cocktail in a bar with a view**. Grab a sundowner at one of New York's many rooftop terraces and marvel at the panoramic view over the city ♿ *p. 114, 115, 116 & 117*.

💚 **Take a break in a pocket park**. Tucked away in one of the city's many pint-sized pocket parks, secluded from the hubbub, you'll hear only birdsong and the sound of running water. An ideal quiet spot for a break. ♿ *p. 66*.

💚 **Follow the stars of the silver screen**. Take the family on a trip to the Museum of the Moving Image in Astoria, Queens. ♿ *p. 100*.

💚 **Go to a gospel service in Harlem** on a Sunday morning. Expect impassioned sermons and rousing song. Finish the morning back on earth with a brunch in the neighborhood. ♿ *p. 126 & 142*.

💚 **Go to an outdoor market in Brooklyn.** Grab a veggie burger and fresh fruit juice and have lunch on the grass while admiring the view of Manhattan. Spend the morning soaking in the hipster Brooklyn vibe and perusing the stalls of vintage clothing, re-purposed furniture and hand-made jewelry. ♿ *p. 123*.

💚 **Pay homage to Frank Lloyd Wright** and the magnificent spiral ramp that has made the Guggenheim Museum recognized the world over. ♿ *p. 80*.

💚 **Recharge in the quiet medieval gardens of the Cloisters**, with a view out over the Hudson River. Your backdrop is the stones of cloisters shipped from Europe and reconstructed stone by stone. ♿ *p. 94*.

💚 **Breathe in the fresh air in Riverside Park.** Abundant nature and great views over the Hudson are on offer. Cycle along the water or go for

6

© JeffreyFina/iStock

The Cloisters

© littleny/iStock

7

Williamsburg Flea

your weekly (annual?) run; children will love the playgrounds and skate parks. Nearby are the Museum of Natural History *p. 86* and Children's Museum of Manhattan.

♥ **Watch the sun set from Tudor City Place at the eastern end of 42nd St.** This is also one of the best spots to contemplate the Chrysler Building. *p. 64*.

♥ **Feel tiny under the 55-ft Barosaurus skeleton at the American Museum of Natural History.** The rich collection here will delight children, taking them on a journey back in time, and is one of the largest of its kind in the world. *p. 86*.

♥ **Bulgogi, barbecue, and karaoke.** Explore Koreatown for delicious eats like smoky Korean barbecue followed by karaoke, or pick up ingredients at one of the Korean supermarkets *p. 56*.

♥ **Visit the Whitney Museum** of American Art, designed by Renzo Piano. The space thrills with its bright modular galleries and terraces on each level, with views over the High Line. *p. 46*.

New York in 3 days

Beyond Manhattan

Take a jaunt to Queens and take in the contemporary art at PSI★ (p. 99), or head to the family-friendly Museum of the Moving Image★★ (p. 100). Fill up at Ornella (p. 111) before hopping over to Brooklyn. Start with a walk in Brooklyn Heights★★ (p. 95), with breathtaking views of Manhattan, then spend the evening discovering the hot spots of Williamsburg★ (p. 110, 117 & 126). Be sure to grab a cocktail at Ides Bar (p. 117), the rooftop bar of the chic and ultra-hip Wythe Hotel.

DAY 1

▶ **Morning**
Start your day by taking in the topography of New York from the top of the **Empire State Building★★★** *(p. 54)* or the **Top of the Rock★★★** *(p. 58)*.

▶ **Midday**
Stop at Café Serai *(p. 108)* in the **Rubin Museum★★** *(p. 46); or* picnic with goods from **Chelsea Market** *(p. 108)*. You can get your food to go and stroll the **High Line★★** *(p. 47)*.

▶ **Afternoon**
Tour the galleries ★★ *(p. 45)* of Chelsea, before exploring **Greenwich Village★★** *(p. 40)* and the **Meatpacking District★** *(p. 45)*.

▶ **Evening**
Stay in Meatpacking for a drink with a view on the terrace of **The Top of The Standard** *(p. 115)* or get dinner in the **Lower East Side★** *(p. 106)*, another trendy neighborhood.

DAY 2

▶ **Morning**
Set off early to get up close to the **Statue of Liberty★★★** *(p. 22)*. When you arrive back in Manhattan, walk into the **Financial District★★** *(p. 20)*.

▶ **Afternoon**
Visit the site of the **World Trade Center★★★** *(p. 14)*. Check out **South Seaport Street Historic District★★** *(p. 26)*, New York's first port, before walking across the **Brooklyn Bridge** *(p. 26)* where the views over Manhattan are unforgettable.

▶ **Evening**
Spend an evening in **Greenwich Village★★** *(p. 42, 106 and 125)*, a lively neighborhood full of great spots to wine and dine.

Where are the clubs?

Club kids can head to Meatpacking and Chelsea, where you'll find veteran nightclubs. Or, for more space and Brooklyn vibes, Nowadays (p. 126) in Ridgewood is totally worth the trek.

© Boogich/iStock

9

High Line

DAY 3

▶*Morning*
Arty morning at the **Met**★★★ *(p. 74)*.
▶*Midday*
Have a picnic under the trees of
Central Park★★★ *(p. 67 & 109)*, or opt
for the Roof Garden Café at the Met.
▶*Afternoon*
Continue your cultured day at the
MoMA★★★ *(p. 58)*. If you still have
energy left and cash in your pocket,
do a spot of shopping between
Madison and **5ᵗʰ Avenue**★★★ *(p. 54)*.
▶*Evening*
Get a little bit of rest before your
night out on **Broadway**★ *(p. 51)*. Catch
a 7pm show and then get lost among
the neon signs of **Times Square**★★

A fourth day?
*Brush up on your painting knowledge
at the **Frick Collection**★★★ (p. 71),
then get lunch at **Barney Greengrass**
(p. 109). In the afternoon, visit the
Museum of Natural History★★★
(p. 86). Alternatively, swap a museum
for a wander in **Riverside Park**★★
(p. 90) or a shopping session in **Soho**★★
(p. 32 and 119). Let your evening
meal transport you with dinner in
Koreatown (p. 56) or **Chinatown**★★
(p. 28 and p. 104).*

(p. 53). For a quick and inexpensive
dinner, indulge in a burger at Shake
Shack *(p. 108)*.

Disovering
New York

11

Central Park in summer
© Jean Pierre Lescourret/hemis.fr

New York today

The writer E. B. White wasn't wrong when he said, "There are roughly three New Yorks. There is, first, the New York of the man or woman who was born here, who takes the city for granted and accepts its size and its turbulence as natural and inevitable. Second, there is the New York of the commuter — the city that is devoured by locusts each day and spat out each night. Third, there is the New York of the person who was born somewhere else and came to New York in quest of something. Commuters give the city its tidal restlessness; natives give it solidity and continuity; but the settlers give it passion."

New York is entirely different from the rest of America. Either way, to come to New York is to experience an **unforgettable shock to the system:** the city leaves no one indifferent. For many, getting lost amid the colorful avenues and boulevards that literature, cinema and music have made so familiar is enough to fall in love with the place immediately, and for life. There is much to charm: crossing the man-made canyons created between the gleaming cliffs of the skyscrapers; soaking in the cosmopolitan ambiance in the old neighborhoods of Chinatown and Harlem; jogging in Central Park; or seeing the skyline of Manhattan suddenly appear across the East River as you cross Brooklyn Bridge

The "vertical city", as French writer Céline called it, is full of paradoxes. The megalopolis overspills with vitality despite the trauma of 9/11. The city is at once coarse and sophisticated, of-the-people and elitist, typically American and still different from any other American city. As for New Yorkers themselves, they consider their city to be beyond doubt the most beautiful, most important and most "everything" city in the world.

It's hard to disagree. The frenetic rhythm of the city will draw you in immediately, making you feel that something important is happening– that you are at the center of the world. It's a **whirlwind** of light, sound and movement. Amid surging cars, howling sirens, incessant construction, whirring air conditioning units and the fractured hubbub of the city, the noise level never really goes down, not even at night (despite the Silent Night initiative brought in by former mayor Michael Bloomberg, which didn't succeed in changing much).

The first visual impression of the city is one of irrepressible vitality, almost aggression. The sharp-lined skyscrapers, one shamelessly out-climbing the next, don't feign any attempt at harmony. The competition and one-upmanship of the cityscape creates a jagged **kaleidoscope** of mismatched shapes with only one aim: do better; build higher, build more expensive. Observers have often characterized this aesthetic as masculine, even phallic: think vertical pillars of concrete and glass that enveloped passers-by in their vast shadow. You can always tell the tourists because they're the only ones looking up as they walk — New Yorkers have better things to do. To discover New York is to go on an **adventure**, immersing yourself in this hyperactive maelstrom of contrasts. The unchanging familiarities of the Old World are forgotten here: the city advances relentlessly, and will continue to do so, whatever comes. If you think you know fast traffic, prepare to think again when you arrive in New York. **Taxi drivers** will not contradict even the most exaggerated Hollywood depictions of their profession; the buses seem to be engaged in a car chase. The pace of the city is undeniable: New Yorkers never stop. The sometimes overwhelming noise in the middle of the night of sirens, construction, and bar-goers will remind you that in this town, every minute counts.

New Yorkers, of course, walk fast. They know where they're going; they're busy; they have three times more things to do than the 24 hours of the day could possibly allow. Make sure you keep pace!

© espiegle/iStock

5th Avenue by Madison Square

On the sidewalk, pedestrians follow one another and walk on the right. This is the only place where everyone does the same thing. Discipline is essential: it's the only way the rush hour hoards can avoid hurting each other.

Now that you have the keys, the rest is up to you. Surviving in the **whirlwind** that is New York can feel like making your way through a jungle. But you will soon start to feel at ease here. After a few short hours, you'll find yourself magically carried along by the city's irrepressible vitality.

Lower Manhattan★★

The city as we know it began right here. The legendary skyline contrasts with old cobbled streets, all punctuated with symbolic sites: the World Trade Center, with its poignant memories; the Brooklyn Bridge; Wall Street and the New York Stock Exchange, the global nucleus of finance and, in the distance, the familiar silhouette of the Statue of Liberty.

Access: Subway: all stations between Chambers St. and South Ferry (lines 1 to 6, E, J, R, W, Z). Bus: M9, M15, M20, M22, M55, M103 all have stops in Lower Manhattan. The red Downtown Connection bus is **free** and runs throughout Lower Manhattan. *www.downtownny.com*

Area map p. 16-17. **Detachable map AB8**.

▶**Tip:** for great photos of the skyscrapers, head to Brooklyn Bridge in the morning. At night, admire the illuminated skyline from Brooklyn Heights. Advance booking is advisable for visiting the Federal Reserve Bank or City Hall.

The first European colonists, the Dutch, settled on the southern tip of Manhattan and established a large farming village. The original layout of that village has been partially conserved, meaning you won't find the city's characteristic grid, but rather streets that run odd angles. The settlement quickly became a busy commercial port, first under **Dutch control** (◔ *p. 152)*, and then English. However, the markets were unstable as a result of ongoing political unrest and violence. In 1792, 16 years after the Declaration of Independence was signed, financiers decided to establish New York's first stock market with the money made from property speculation. You'll still find vestiges of the early city at Fraunces Tavern, James Watson House and Trinity Church, and a few remaining cobbled streets. On the other end of the spectrum, the New World Trade Center is a powerful reminder of the tragedy of September 11th.

WORLD TRADE CENTER★★★

New York and the United States changed forever on **September 11, 2001**, when two planes, hijacked and rerouted by terrorists, crashed into the twin towers of the **World Trade Center**. One hour and forty minutes later, they collapsed on themselves; the world looked on horrified as the proudest symbols of American prosperity were swallowed up in a cloud of dust.

Two 110-story structures disappeared, taking with them 2973 victims.

Statue of Liberty and Lower Manhattan skyline

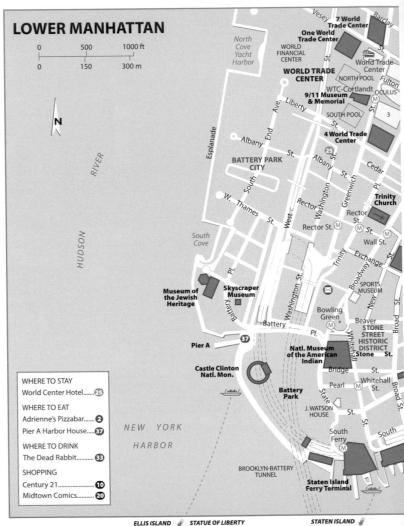

LOWER MANHATTAN

```
0        500      1000 ft
0    150     300 m
```

N

HUDSON RIVER

North Cove Yacht Harbor

WORLD FINANCIAL CENTER

Vesey
7 World Trade Center
Barclay
One World Trade Center
World Trade Center
WORLD TRADE CENTER
NORTH POOL
Fulton
WTC-Cortlandt
OCULUS
9/11 Museum & Memorial
SOUTH POOL
Liberty
3
St.
4 World Trade Center
Albany
Esplanade
End
Ave.
Cedar
South
W. Thames St.
West
BATTERY PARK CITY
Rector
Washington
Greenwich
Trinity Church
Rector St. (M)
Rector St.
South Cove
Wall St.
Exchange
Trinity
Broadway
SPORTS MUSEUM
New
Broad St.
Museum of the Jewish Heritage
Skyscraper Museum
Washington St.
Bowling Green
Battery
Beaver
STONE STREET HISTORIC DISTRICT
Stone St.
Pier A
Battery Pl.
Natl. Museum of the American Indian
Bridge St.
Whitehall St.
Castle Clinton Natl. Mon.
Pearl
Battery Park
J. WATSON HOUSE
State
St.
South
Broad St.
NEW YORK HARBOR
South Ferry (M)
BROOKLYN-BATTERY TUNNEL
Staten Island Ferry Terminal

WHERE TO STAY	
World Center Hotel	25
WHERE TO EAT	
Adrienne's Pizzabar	2
Pier A Harbor House	37
WHERE TO DRINK	
The Dead Rabbit	33
SHOPPING	
Century 21	10
Midtown Comics	20

16

ELLIS ISLAND   STATUE OF LIBERTY   STATEN ISLAND

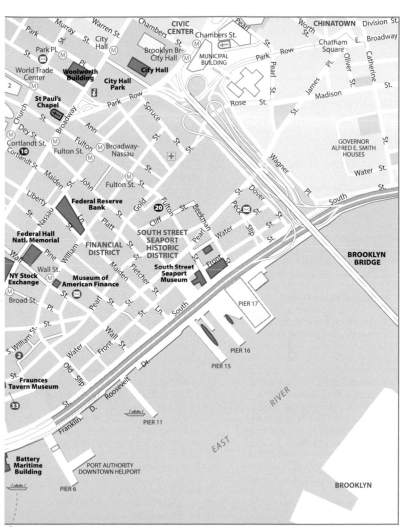

CHINATOWN

Division St.

CIVIC CENTER

Chambers St.

Murray St.

Warren St.

Park Pl.

City Hall Pl.

MUNICIPAL BUILDING

Worth St.

Chatham Square

E. Broadway

Catherine St.

Oliver St.

James St.

Madison St.

World Trade Center

Woolworth Building

City Hall

Brooklyn Br-City Hall

Pearl St.

Park Row

Row

St. Paul's Chapel

City Hall Park

Rose St.

Pearl St.

Church St.

Broadway

Ann St.

Park Row

Spruce St.

GOVERNOR ALFRED E. SMITH HOUSES

Dey St.

Fulton St.

Broadway-Nassau

Water St.

Cortlandt St.

Maiden Ln.

John St.

Fulton St.

Wagner Pl.

South St.

Water St.

Liberty St.

Federal Reserve Bank

Gold St.

Fulton St.

Cliff St.

Dover St.

Peck Slip

Nassau St.

Platt St.

SOUTH STREET SEAPORT HISTORIC DISTRICT

Beekman St.

Water St.

South St.

Federal Hall Natl. Memorial

FINANCIAL DISTRICT

William St.

Pine St.

Maiden Ln.

Fletcher St.

Pearl St.

Front St.

BROOKLYN BRIDGE

17

NY Stock Exchange

Museum of American Finance

Wall St.

South Street Seaport Museum

Broad St.

Pearl St.

South St.

PIER 17

S. William St.

Wall St.

Water St.

Front St.

South St.

PIER 16

Fraunces Tavern Museum

Old Slip

Roosevelt Dr.

PIER 15

EAST RIVER

Franklin D. Roosevelt Dr.

PIER 11

Battery Maritime Building

EAST

PORT AUTHORITY DOWNTOWN HELIPORT

BROOKLYN

PIER 6

GOVERNOR'S ISLAND

Finished in 1973, after eleven years of construction works, the towers rose to 411m/1348ft (more or less double the height of all the surrounding towers) and accounted for 16% of the office space in Downtown. Around 50 000 people worked there.

The project – None of the proposed projects, even the one that was eventually taken up, proved to be entirely satisfactory. The initial plans of **Daniel Libeskind** were modified by the architect **David Childs**, so much so that the first stone, laid with great pomp in 2004, had to be replaced in 2006. There will be six new towers in the place of the seven buildings destroyed in the attacks, with building works slated to finish in 2020. The south-east of the site offers the best view of the ongoing construction and best vantage point to take in its enormous size. On the corner of **Church and Vesey Streets**, parts of each tower are preserved behind high railings with sober plaques referring to the tragedy. **One World Trade Center** (1 WTC), formerly Freedom Tower, stands at 541m/1776ft, a reference to the date of the Independence of the United States. Today it stands alongside 7 WTC (inaugurated in 2006), 4 WTC (inaugurated in 2013) and 3 WTC (inaugurated in 2018), and will soon be neighbored by 5 WTC (130 Liberty St.), 2 WTC (200 Greenwich St. – completion slated for 2024). 2 WTC will be the city's second largest skyscraper and will feature a diamond-shaped roof. **One World Observatory**★★★ – One World Trade Center - 285 Fulton St. - ☎ 212 602 4000 - www.oneworld

observatory.com - daily hours vary: check website for details (last tickets sold 45min before closing) - $40 (over 65s $38, 6-12 years $34). The observatory on the 102nd fl. is reached by one of the fastest elevators in the world: during the ascent (57 seconds) the evolution of the Manhattan skyline from 17C to present, is retraced on the walls of the elevator. From the top, the 360°-view over Manhattan, 380m/1247ft up, is breathtaking. On a clear day, the view stretches 80km/50mi in every direction. The view will help you get a feel for the geography of the city, with its long spits of land, hemmed in by water.

9/11 Museum & Memorial★★ – 180 Greenwich St. (corner of Dey St.) - ☎ 212 312 8800 - www.911memorial. org - museum: Sun-Thur 9am-8pm last entry at 6pm), Fri-Sat 9am-9pm (last entry at 7pm); memorial : daily 7.30am-9pm hours subject to variation, check online before your visit - advance booking essential (online) - $ 26 ($20 over 65s and students, $15/7-12 years). The underground museum takes you into the guts of the WTC. Here, thousands of artifacts related to the tragedy are exhibited, spanning objects such as a partially-burned ID card and a fire truck melted out of shape by the unimaginable heat. Photos and videos punctuate the visit and homage is paid to each of the 2973 victims killed in the attacks. Visitors can listen to various impossibly heartbreaking sound recordings, including the deeply affecting messages left by future victims, stuck in the burning towers or on the planes.

The management of the museum, however, have also faced some criticism. There were accusations that the exhibits did not present the global geopolitical situation seriously enough; there was also controversy surrounding the decision to include a gift shop, which many found inappropriate. Most contentiously, there were mixed reactions following the decision to place the unidentified remains of victims on the site, in the bedrock 70ft (21m) below ground. The memorial, *Reflecting the Absence*, by architect **Michael Arad**, is made up of two 9m/30ft-deep pools down which run vast man-made waterfalls. They are surrounded by bronze panels engraved with the names of each of the victims. More than 400 oak trees are planted around the basins, giving the site a calm and serene atmosphere, conducive to quiet contemplation.

One tree distinguishes itself from the others: a pear tree, recovered from the debris after the attacks. Today, visitors gather round it to touch the bark of the "miracle tree", a symbol of hope and regeneration.

Station – Also called the Oculus, the World Trade Center station was designed by Santiago Calatrava. Recognizable by its vast steel wings, it welcomes an estimated 250 000 people daily, and features a shopping center and dining options.

CITY HALL★

www.nyc.gov - tours by reservation only on select dates (📞 212 788 2656; tours@cityhall.nyc.gov).

Recognizable by its high clock tower, City Hall is one of New York's most elegant buildings. Its Georgian interior (1812) is housed behind a fine marble facade, inspired by the French Renaissance. The architects, not knowing the city would spread north, made the back of the building in brown sandstone; it was only in 1956 that it was covered in Alabama limestone. Right outside is the **City Hall Park**. It was here in what was a field of apple trees that the Declaration of Independence was read in July 1776.

WOOLWORTH BUILDING★★

233 Broadway. - 📞 203 966 9663 - woolworthtours.com - guided lobby tour 1hr on select dates (reservations must be made online) - $30.
Erected in 1913 by architect **Cass Gilbert** for **Frank Woolworth**, who owned a large chain of shops, this 241m/790ft edifice would remain until 1930 the world's tallest skyscraper, when the Chrysler Building was completed. With its stunning profusion of gargoyles and pinnacles and green clock-tower-adorned roof, it's considered one of the city's greatest architectural works. Its spectacular lobby mixes Gothic and Byzantine frescoes and mosaics.

SAINT PAUL'S CHAPEL

209 Broadway - 📞 212 602 0800 - 10am-6pm (opens 11am on Wed.), services Sunday 8am, 9.15am and 11.15am.

Wall Street

Wall Street emerged as an important financial center in the 19C; in 1920, it became the world's leading stock exchange, ahead of London. It has not been surpassed since, despite the crashes of 1929, 1987 and 2008. In the wake of these crises, many office buildings were left unoccupied and turned into housing.

New York Stock Exchange (NYSE) – This elegant 17-storey edifice (1903) houses the New York Stock Exchange. It is constructed in the style of a classical temple, with Corinthian columns and a pediment featuring allegorical sculpted figures representing commerce.

Stone Street Historic District★ – Between Wall Street and the East River, this was the first paved road in Manhattan. A protected site since 1996, it has conserved its old-world charm with its brick buildings crisscrossed with painted metal staircases and contemporary happy hour bars.

Federal Hall National Memorial★ – *26 Wall St. - ℘ 212 825 6990 - www. nps.gov/feha - daily except weekends 9am-5pm - closed Thanksgiving, Christmas, and New Year's Day - free.* Located close to the NYSE, this edifice in the style of a temple is built on the site of New York's first City Hall, constructed in 1699 and then used as a law court. Redesigned after Independence, it became **Federal Hall**, the headquarters of the first United States Congress. It is here that George Washington was sworn in as president, a scene acted out by his statue here. The current building, which dates from 1842, housed US Customs and then the Treasury.

The oldest church in Manhattan (1766), constructed in the Georgian style popular in London at the time. Fire fighters and rescue workers came here to rest and clean up following the attacks on the World Trade Center.

FINANCIAL DISTRICT★★

Wall Street – It takes its name from the wall that protected the Dutch settlement. Knocked down by the English in 1699, it was replaced by a road which would become the emblem of American capitalism. Lined by beautiful Georgian buildings,

© P. Adams/Danita Delimont Agency/age fotostock

FEDERAL RESERVE BANK★

33 Liberty St. - www.newyorkfed. org - guided tour 1hr - recommended booking approx. 1 month in advance- Mon-Fri 1pm and 2pm except public holidays - arrive 30min before - valid ID essential - free.

The austere facade as well as the railings on its windows and its sober lobby emphasize the importance of its function. It plays the hugely consequential role of establishing US monetary policy, and therefore influencing the world economy. The vault, buried more than 24m/79ft below street level, and 15m/49ft under sea level, houses billions of dollars of gold reserves belonging to the US and the central banks of approximately sixty countries; the contents constitute 25-30% of the world's reserves and it is the world's largest single reserve (more than 10 000t).

TRINITY CHURCH★

75 Broadway (at Wall St.) - www. trinitywallstreet.org - 7am-6pm - , services Sunday 9am and weekdays 12.05pm - concerts on select days, consult website for info.

Built in 1846, this was once the highest monument in New York. Its imposing neo-Gothic red sandstone facade was relatively unscathed by the collapse of the World Trade Center, despite being so close. Listen for the twelve change-ringing bells (the only set in USA) on Sundays. The cemetery contains 17C tombs, including the gravesite of Alexander Hamilton.

MUSEUM OF JEWISH HERITAGE★★

Ⓜ *line 1 (stations South Ferry or Rector Street), lines 4 and 5 (station Bowling Green) or line R (stations Whitehall Street or Rector Street. 36 Battery Place - ℘ 646 437 4202 - www.mjhnyc.org - Sun-Fri 10am-6pm (Wed 9pm, Fri 5pm and 3pm Nov- March) - closed Thanksgiving and Jewish festivals - $16 timed tickets, $25 flexible tickets ($12 over 65s, $10 students) - Allow 1hr.*

The understated grace of the building and well-curated exhibits make this a fascinating museum of Jewish history. The six sides of the building and six-tiered roof are a tribute to the six million Jewish people who died in the Holocaust and the six points of the Star of David. The documents presented, including the particularly moving **Klarsfeld Pillars**, tell the story of the Holocaust, Jewish immigration to the US and the revival of Judaism. The café offers one of the finest views of the harbor.

STATUE OF LIBERTY★★★

Access to the pier where the boat departs by Ⓜ lines 4 and 5 (Bowling Green) or line R (Whitehall Street). A ferry departing from the adjacent pier at Castle Clinton (ticket office) serves the Statue of Liberty, then Ellis Island. Statue Cruises – ℘ 877 523 9849 - www.statuecruises.com - June-Sep: departures every 25min from 8.30am to 5pm (4pm in Sept.); rest of the year: dep. every 25min from 9.20am to 3.30pm - combined ticket for the

Statue of Liberty and Ellis Island: statue pedestal $19.25 (4-12 years $9), statue crown $22.25 (4-12 years $12) - incl. audio guide - free tours given by park rangers.

A symbol of the friendship between the US and France since the American Revolution, the Statue of Liberty remains one of the country's icons; Sculptor **Frédéric Auguste Bartholdi** chose liberty to symbolize entry into the New World and to signal to the world the importance of this principle. In 1884, the statue, financed and constructed in Paris by the French, was presented to the American ambassador, then deconstructed to be taken across the Atlantic.

The American funds collected thanks to the public solicitations of *New York World* publisher **Joseph Pulitzer** facilitated the construction of the pedestal. The statue reached New York in June 1885 and was inaugurated on October 28, 1886. The story goes that Bartholdi gave the statue the body of his wife and the face of his mother. He first made a plaster model, then enlisted **Gustave Eiffel** to construct an interior skeleton of iron and steel, weighing 125 tons. The architect covered it in 300 copper plates to create the statue's green "skin". Lady Liberty measures more than 45m/147ft from the base to the torch. A person could be clasped in its hand (4.8m/15.7ft-long) and its foot would easily crush any unfortunate soul. The gold-plated torch was replaced during a 1980s renovation.

ELLIS ISLAND★★
AND IMMIGRATION MUSEUM★★

www.nps.gov/elis. When you arrive, go straight to the information desk to get your tickets for the film; sessions fill up quickly.

Ellis Island was chosen, in 1892 as the entrance point to the United States for immigrants from Europe. The Art Nouveau style building where they were registered now houses documents and artifacts relating the conditions and experiences of the millions of immigrants who passed through here; some were accepted, some pushed back, and all would have waited hours or even days. The center closed in 1954. After the film, opt for a free guided tour with a park ranger. that departs on the hour from the information desk.

BATTERY PARK

Before arrival of the Dutch (**☾** *p. 152*), the southern tip of Manhattan was covered in marshland. The strip that forms today's Battery Park and the piers was reclaimed from the sea. The park is named after the two artillery batteries installed there during the War of 1812. The first is located on Governors Island (**☾** *p. 24*); the second, Castle Clinton (**☾** *p. 24*), occupied another islet 100m/328ft from the river bank. In 1870, the passage between the river bank and Castle Clinton was filled, creating the current arrangement of Battery Park. From the **promenade★**, you will see the Statue of Liberty, Ellis Island and the banks of New Jersey.

Ellis Island Immigration Museum
© René Mattes/hemis.fr

Castle Clinton – ✆ 212 344 7220 - *www.nps.gov/cacl - 7.45am-5pm, guided tours (30min) daily at 10am, 12pm, 2pm, 4pm - free.* This small circular fort, which once housed an artillery battery, was converted in 1821 into an opera house and theater, the **Castle Garden**. It then served as a welcome center for new immigrants (1855-1890) before the construction of the site on Ellis Island. In 34 years, more than eight million people passed through its doors. From 1896 to 1941, it housed the New York City Aquarium.

Pier A★ – The oldest pier in Manhattan, a venerable Victorian-style structure, punctuated by a clock-tower. At the foot of Pier A, the **American Merchant Marine Memorial** pays homage to the shipwrecked of a boat torpedoed during the Second World War.

NATIONAL MUSEUM OF THE AMERICAN INDIAN★★

1 Bowling Green - www.american indian.si.edu - 10am-5pm (Thur 8pm) - free.
The museum, housed in the imposing customs building (1907) conceived by Cass Gilbert, features an elliptical rotunda adorned in frescoes by New York painter Reginald Marsh (1898-1954). Created in 1994 by the Smithsonian Institution, the museum is dedicated to the presentation and preservation of Native American culture, both historical and contemporary. The museum also organizes film projections, concerts and dance performances.

STATEN ISLAND FERRY★★

At the end of Whitehall St. - www. siferry.com - every 30min in the day, every 15min during rush hour (7am-9am and 5pm-7pm), once an hour at night between 1.30am and 5.30am - 25min crossing, allow 1hr30min for just the journey there and back - times are subject to variation, check online before your trip - pedestrians and bikes only - free.
Wrap up warm — it can get very cold out on the water! On the journey there, position yourself on the right to get a view of the Statue of Liberty. On the way back, head to the front of the ferry to see Manhattan coming into view. Around 20 million people use this ferry every year, of which most are commuters going to work. For tourists, it's a unique and free way to enjoy some stunning **views** of the city.

BATTERY MARITIME BUILDING★

11 South St., at the end of Whitehall St. - www.batterymaritimebuilding.com.
This pretty Art Nouveau building (1909) has been entirely restored, with the original colors of its cast iron facade brought back to life. Up until 1938 the Brooklyn Ferry service operated from the terminal. Today it provides a summer ferry service to Governors Island.

Governors Island – *govisland.com - open daily May-Oct. 10am–6pm (Sat-Sun 7pm) - ferry departs Manhattan hourly on weekdays (last ferry from Manhattan 4.15pm, from Governors Island 6pm), and every 20mins on weekends (last ferry from Manhattan*

5.30pm, from Governors Island 7pm)
- $3 (Under 12s free, all passengers
ride free on weekends before noon).
What was once an active military
base since the first fort, Fort Jay, was
built in 1775, is now a popular summer
spot open to the public. The park
went through major redesigns from
2014 to 2016, and now houses artist
residencies, community farm spaces,
and public playgrounds. The annual
Jazz Age Lawn Party in August
sells out every year as dressed-up
partygoers flock to the island for an
evening of music and revelry. You
don't need a ticket to people watch.

FRAUNCES TAVERN MUSEUM★

*54 Pearl St. - ☎ 212 425 1778 -
www.frauncestavernmuseum.org -
Mon-Fri 12pm-5pm, Sat-Sun 11am-5pm
- $7 (over 65s, students, and
6-17years $4) - free guided tours Thur.
and Sun. 1pm, Fri-Sat 1pm and 2pm*
This key site in the American
Revolution was originally the
residence of a rich merchant. before
Samuel Fraunces bought it in 1762
and turned it into a tavern. A group
who met here were the **Sons of
Liberty**, a clandestine organization
of American citizens at the end of the

© mshch/iStock

25

Staten Island Ferry

18C who resisted British repression
during the rebellion of the Thirteen
Colonies against English rule. **George
Washington** would celebrate victory
over the English here. It was also the
site of many political meetings when
New York was the capital. It was
completely restored at the start of the
20C. Its rooms present documents on
the history of Independence.

Brooklyn Bridge in numbers

*For 20 years it was the longest suspension bridge in the world. Construction lasted 14
years and cost $25 million ; 27 perished during its construction. The steel central span,
486m/1594ft long, is supported by two pylons which sink into the water of the East River,
41m/134ft below. The two archways culminate almost 48m/157ft above the deck of the
bridge. The main suspension cables are 40cm/15.7in thick. The pedestrian walkway, at
the top of the structure, was reconstructed between 1981 and 1983.*

SOUTH STREET SEAPORT HISTORIC DISTRICT★★

Situated to the south of Brooklyn Bridge, the **Port of New York**, founded in the 17C, was the first driver of the city's economy. Piers, warehouses and trading houses would gain influence as international commerce developed. The creation of a ferry line between Fulton Street and Brooklyn (1814), the opening of **Fulton Market** (1822) (the former fish market has been converted into a commercial and entertainment center), and the creation of the Erie Canal in 1825 would turn this into an area buzzing with activity. During the second half of the 19C, however, the **East River** would see maritime traffic decrease, with more going to the new piers in the deep waters of the **Hudson River**. It was only after 1967, when the area was designated a historic district, that the port slowly began to regain its appeal, offering a taste of the atmosphere of the beginning of New York.

SOUTH STREET SEAPORT MUSEUM★

12 Fulton St. - ☎ 212 748 8600 - www.southstreetseaportmuseum. org - Wed-Sun 11am-5pm to visit the exhibits on board the legendary boats (weather permitting)- $20 (obver 65s and students $14, under 9s free) May-Oct: 2-hour cruises ($32). The museum houses a significant collection of models, instruments and documents, as well as a collection of old ships along Piers 15 and 16,

the most spectacular being the 1885 cargo ship *Wavertree* and the 1907 Lightship *Ambrose.* The visit can be carried on to **Fulton Street★** and **Water Street★**, commercial streets restored to early 19C style, with some quaint old-fashioned shops. **Bowne & Co. Stationers** is a 19C-style print shop with working historic printing presses from the museum's collection — a great spot to pick up souvenirs.

BROOKLYN BRIDGE★★★

This is a testament to the technical prowess of the 19C. This iconic suspension bridge linking Manhattan to Brooklyn was inaugurated in May 1883. Before its construction, around 50 million people would take the ferry every year to cross the East River. Conceived by **John Augustus Roebling**, the architect of the suspension bridge over Niagara Falls, it was made by his son who drew inspiration from new European techniques. For the construction of its foundations, workers were submerged in wooden chambers pumped with compressed air, but the system lacked some refinement and many of them suffered from burst eardrums. The bridge is a masterpiece of aesthetics and engineering, featuring a central pedestrian walkway elevated above the traffic and neolithic granite archways amid vast network of cables. The **views** over Manhattan and the port are spectacular. Note that in nice weather, the pedestrian walkway can be very crowded. Watch out for cyclists.

Pier 15, South Street Seaport

Chinatown★★, Little Italy and Nolita

In bustling **Chinatown,** *sights and smells assail the senses. Of the infamous* **Little Italy,** *where once upon a time mafia Godfathers dictated the law, only the prosciutto and parmesan remain.* **Nolita** *has become a super trendy extension of Soho.*

▶**Access:** Subway: Canal St., Spring St., Prince St., Grand St. and Broadway-Lafayette. Bus: M21, M55, M1.

Area maps p. 31 and 36. Detachable map BC7.

▶**Tips:** Visit Chinatown in the morning when the streets are not yet too packed, then wander through Little Italy to Nolita, lively in the afternoons and evenings.

CHINATOWN★★

Chinese immigration to New York started in the 1870s. A decade later, this area was known for brothels, gambling houses and opium dens. Today, the Chinese population of Chinatown is 200 000, making it one of the largest such communities outside of Asia. Shops filled with gadgets are interspersed with tea sellers and purveyors of Eastern medicine, as well as a few trendy restaurants and cafés. On Canal St. are an abundance of designer imitations.

Museum of Chinese in America (MOCA) – *215 Centre St. (corner of Grand St.) - ℘ 212 619 4785 - www. mocanyc.org - daily except Mon 11am-6pm (Thur. 9pm) - $ 12 (over 65s and students $8, under 2s free).* This modern museum explores the ways of life of the Chinese diaspora in America.

LITTLE ITALY

The first Italian immigrants grouped together in this area which quickly became a hotbed of organized crime, controlled by the Mafia. Today, Little Italy has lost most of its Italians to other neighborhoods, but it's still a lovely area for a stroll. Box-set fans may happily recognize **Mulberry Street Café** *(no. 176)*, backdrop of much-loved series *The Sopranos*.

NOLITA

Cafés, little restaurants and trendy boutiques are sprinkled across the northern part of Little Italy's leafy streets (Nolita = "North of Little Italy"). **The Basilica of St. Patrick's Old Cathedral**, in neo-Gothic style (1815), was until 1879 the Catholic cathedral of New York.

Tribeca★★ and Soho★★

Tribeca *offers a happy mix of chic restaurants, warehouses converted into pricey lofts and art galleries. Beyond its luxury boutiques, charming delis and hyped bars,* **Soho** *is home to some of the most beautifully preserved cast iron architecture in the country. It was taken over by artists in the 1960s, and then inevitably became too expensive for the bohemians; today it's a haven for yuppies.*

▶**Access:** Subway Chambers St., Franklyn St. and Canal St. for Tribeca; Houston St., Broadway-Lafayette, Spring St. and Canal St. for Soho.
Area map p. 31*. **Detachable map AB7***.
▶**Tip:** if you're an art lover, you will get a lot from wandering Tribeca, with the New York Gallery Guide in tow (www.artdealers.org/gallery-guide). Note that galleries are closed on Sundays and Mondays. If shopping is more your bag, head for Soho (boutiques open from 10am). There is much to please **architecture aficionados** in both areas.

TRIBECA★★

The name of the area comes from the contraction of **TRI**angle **BE**low **CA**nal, though technically it is more trapeze-shaped. At the start of the 18C, this section of town housed the residences of rich families. It was only in the middle of the 19C, when the quays of the Hudson River supplanted South Street Seaport, that warehouses would fill the area. This was the great era of **cast-iron architecture** and brick; typically structures were built five or six floors high and housed offices or stockrooms. On the eve of the Second World War, this was one of the city's most industrious areas, bringing together manufacturing, services and trade. But during the

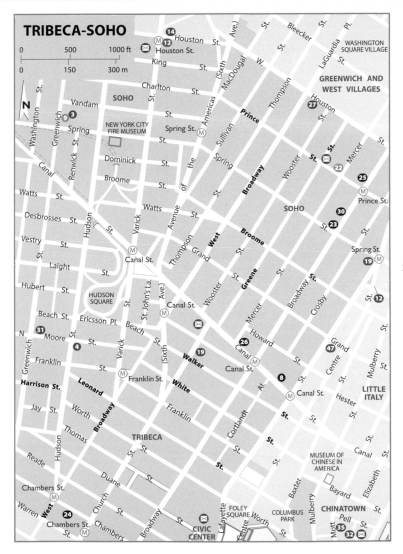

TRIBECA-SOHO

1960s, Tribeca saw a slow and painful fall in desirability, triggered by the decline in manufacturing and of the port. In 1970, Tribeca and its worn-out buildings were home to only 243 inhabitants.

The area was saved by the large number of artists pushed out of Soho by rocketing prices; creative types emigrated here and converted the warehouses and workshops into art galleries. Today, with a population of more than 10,000, including a number of celebrities (Robert De Niro, in particular, is known for his investment in the life of Tribeca), this neighborhood has become highly desirable once more. As you explore the area, be sure to pass by **Washington Market Park**, which was once one of the most active markets in New York. **Harrison Street**, a row of houses in Federal style, built between 1796 and 1828, gives an idea of what Tribeca would have looked like at this time. On **Leonard Street**, you'll find a number of imposing buildings such as the Clock Tower Building (headquarters of the New York Life Insurance Company) which features the last active mechanical clock in the city. Between **West Broadway** and Broadway you'll find the typical urban architecture of the 19C, with its brick facades in varying colors and its sets of cast iron columns. **White Street** is a fine example. **Tribeca Synagogue** is recognizable by its distinctive curved shape. On **Walker Street** you'll find various galleries and artists' studios. To the west, the **AT & T Headquarters Building** is an example of the popular New York Art Deco style. Built in 1918,

it features a spectacular lobby with stunning mosaics.

The area's latest icon, **56 Leonard Street,** designed by Swiss architects Herzog & de Meuron, stuns with its original design, resembling a number of irregular sized boxes stacked on top of each other.

In the last fifteen years, under the patronage of Robert De Niro, Tribeca has become the epicenter of New York cinema. In 2002, the actor created the **Tribeca Film Festival** with film producer Jane Rosenthal. The thinking was that New York deserved a noteworthy festival and that it would help breathe new life into the area, which was badly affected by September 11 attacks. The festival is not short on quality films and attendees; a selection of the world's best films are projected in various theaters across the area.

SOHO★★

Soho (**SO**uth of **HO**uston St) is one of the chicest areas in New York, with its boutiques, restaurants and art galleries. The neighborhood's history is quite varied.

In 1644, this area was home to Manhattan's first black community, a group of freed slaves. At the start of the 19C, wealthy bourgeois like James Fenimore Cooper, author of *The Last of the Mohicans*, began moving into the area.

Situated between the business-orientated Lower Manhattan in the south, and the large, elegant mansions of the north, Soho became one of the most densely populated

Soho

parts of town. Theaters, hotels, restaurants, casinos and shops were opened along **Broadway** and the surrounding streets. To please revelers, **Mercer Street** became a hub for brothels, with two thirds of New York's sex workers here at one point. Displeased by its evolution, the bourgeois eventually left Soho for the neighborhoods farther north, while the most prosperous commerces would move up to 5th Avenue. During the second half of the 19C, residences were slowly replaced by businesses, offices and warehouses. Architects began to employ a new construction technique: **cast iron architecture**. Developed by the English at the end of the 18C, it allowed for rapid construction and new architectural styles. The lighter facades featured more windows. The cast iron elements, created in molds and reproduced in large quantity, could be combined in different combinations, according to building sizes and client demands. The final construction was then painted. The result was whole streets lined with graceful colonnades, elegant cornicing and delicate pastel-painted pediments. Today, of the 400 cast irons in the city, some 300 can be found in Soho.

In the 20C, Soho became progressively neglected before being readopted by artist types, drawn by the huge lofts and vast, vacant warehouse spaces. There was an animated campaign to save the area's facades, and in 1973, Soho was classified as a historic district, after which it became the center of contemporary art in New York. Prices subsequently sky-rocketed, causing an exodus of artists and galleries to Chelsea. The creative, vibrant and bohemian feel of the neighborhood made way for the strings of high-end boutiques you see today.

Broadway – In this part of town, Broadway is not associated with theaters, but rather is a hub for commerce and shopping. Note the stunning **Silk Exchange Building** (1895) at *487 Broadway*. The finely constructed building features an Italianized Rococo facade. On the northwest corner of Prince Street, **the Prada building** (no. 575) sets the tone: from 1991-2001 the site of the Guggenheim Soho, it now features elegant décor designed by architect Rem Koolhaas (**⚑** *Prada, p. 119*). The inauguration of the twelve-floor **Little Singer Building** (nos. 561-563), designed by Ernest Flagg in 1903, with its typically Beaux-Arts style heralded a new era for skyscrapers. It is easily recognizable by its lacy wrought iron floral motifs and long windows The **E.V. Haughwout Building** (nos. 488-492), considered in its time (1857) a veritable "Venetian palace", with its arcades, balustrades and Corinthian columns, was the city's first building with a cast iron facade and the first to have an elevator, installed by Elisha G. Otis.

Greene Street★ – You'll find the largest grouping of cast iron facades on this street. The two most interesting structures, designed by Isaac F. Duckworth in 1872 in Second Empire style, are nicknamed the **King** and **Queen of Greene Street** (nos. 72-76 and 28-30); the former features a grand porch supported by high columns; the latter a mansard roof with elaborate dormer windows.

Prince Street – Peppered with boutiques and art galleries, Prince Street houses a cast iron edifice featuring a *trompe-l'œil* brick wall facade: the work was created by the painter Richard Haas in 1975.

Broome Street – On the corner of Greene Street you'll find the **Gunther Building** (nos. 469-475), a beautiful wrought iron creation from 1873; see also the elegant building at *no. 448*.

West Broadway – Window shop contemporary art and luxury boutiques (Armani, Elie Tahari, Dolce & Gabbana).

Judd Foundation – *101 Spring St. - ☏ 212 219 2747 - juddfoundation. org - Tue-Fri 1pm-6pm, Sat. 11am-6pm -guided tour (90min), advanced reservations required - $24 (over 65s and students $11.50).* The former home and studio of American artist Donald Judd in a sprawling cast iron building. The tour takes visitors through gallery spaces, the kitchen and dining areas, his studio and finally his bedroom on the fifth floor. Art (and furniture) by Judd himself and his contemporaries fill each floor.

Lower East Side★

*Sunday morning is the best time to come and wander here,
perusing the tempting shops selling everything from delicious, crusty bagels
to bohemian blouses. The Lower East Side (LES) was the entry point for
immigrants to New York, who lived crammed together in tenement buildings.
The area has retained a touch of its former shabby look, but the murky buildings
covered in graffiti belie the now-pricey area's incarnation as an ultra-hip district
day and night. The bars, clubs and restaurants of the area blend chic, modern
décor and natty knick-knacks. In the small hours, revelers dance to blues, rock
and electro.*

▶**Access:** Subway: Delancey Street, Essex Street, Grand Street, 2nd Avenue. Bus:
M14A-SBS, M15, M9.
***Area map p. 36**. **Detachable map BC7**.*
▶**Tip:** Head to the Lower East Side on a Sunday. Start with brunch, and then
wander on Orchard Street (shops closed until 10-11am). This is great area for
dinner. New bars and restaurants open constantly. Pick somewhere that looks
interesting and is full, and give it a go. Avoid Saturdays (the Sabbath) as some
businesses may be closed.

In the late 19C and early 20C, the Lower East Side, inexpensive and diverse, was the area of new arrivals, a sort of holding room between their country of origin and vast New York. At one time, the Lower East Side was the most densely populated zone in the world. From 1820, communities of freed **blacks** and **Irish** grouped together in the area, as well as a significant **Chinese community**, working on the construction of railroads. Chased out of their country by famine after 1840, the **Irish** arrived in the hundreds of millions during the 19C, joined by **Germans** fleeing war and religious persecution. The first wave of **Jewish immigration**, from Germany, was followed by the arrival of Jews from Russia and Poland who were fleeing pogroms. **Italians** came across in the second half of the 19C, settling near the Irish and founding Little Italy. Finally **Puerto Ricans** would move in to the area at the end of the 19C and during the first half of the 20C. Though there is still a small Jewish community here, evidenced by the synagogues and a few shops and restaurants, the last immigrant populations still living here are principally Latinos and people of Asian origin. Today, LES is increasingly losing its idiosyncratic character, as it has become one of the trendiest going-out spots for the young, hip crowd. However, there are still traces of its history: though

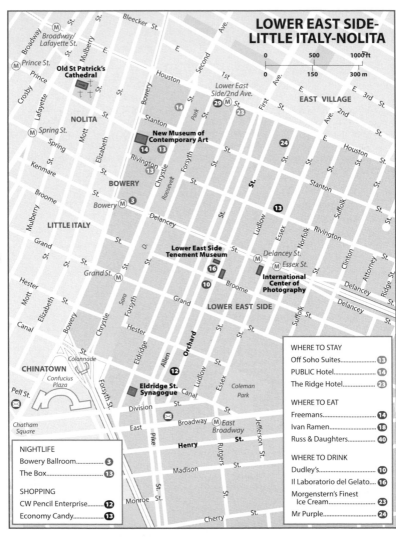

LOWER EAST SIDE-
LITTLE ITALY-NOLITA

EAST VILLAGE

NOLITA

Old St Patrick's
Cathedral

New Museum of
Contemporary Art

BOWERY

LITTLE ITALY

Lower East Side
Tenement Museum

International
Center of
Photography

LOWER EAST SIDE

CHINATOWN

Confucius
Plaza

Eldridge St.
Synagogue

0   500   1000 ft
0   150   300 m

WHERE TO STAY
Off Soho Suites 13
PUBLIC Hotel 14
The Ridge Hotel 23

WHERE TO EAT
Freemans 14
Ivan Ramen 18
Russ & Daughters 40

WHERE TO DRINK
Dudley's 10
Il Laboratorio del Gelato 16
Morgenstern's Finest
  Ice Cream 23
Mr Purple 24

NIGHTLIFE
Bowery Ballroom 3
The Box 13

SHOPPING
CW Pencil Enterprise 12
Economy Candy 13

Couture and cigars

The garment making business of New York began in the Lower East Side, where young women worked in their homes. The cheap cost and ready availability of labor then lead to the establishment of shared workshops. This area also produced cigars in an industry that was directed by Puerto Ricans, with many immigrants from the Caribbean working here.

many buildings have been razed, some streets still retain a bit of the atmosphere of a bygone New York, with old-fashioned shops and cafés and the distinctive brick buildings with narrow windows and iron fire escapes. Their future is not assured, however, as prices continue to rise, and new restaurants and luxury hotels open constantly, attracting an ever-more wealthy clientèle. Nevertheless, you can still discover some authentic charm by wandering **Ludlow Street★** and **Orchard Street,** stopping for a snack in one of the Jewish delis along the way.

The southern part of Orchard Street is occupied by shops selling cheap clothes and leather luggage, some inexpensive tailors and a few upholsters' and decorators' workshops; the northern part is dominated by chic boutiques and restaurants.

© Andrew Pini/Photolibrary/Getty Images

Russ & Daughters — Jewish deli on 179 E. Houston Street

NEW MUSEUM OF CONTEMPORARY ART★

235 Bowery - ☏ 212 219 1222 - www.newmuseum.org - Tue-Sat 11am-6pm (Thur. 9pm) - $18, pay what you wish Thur - 7-9pm. Small gift shop and pleasant café on the ground floor.

Japanese architects Kazuyo Sejima and Ryue Nishizawa/ SANAA designed an accumulation of zinc cubes that seem to only just be balancing, maybe as if to demonstrate the unstable nature of contemporary art. The museum houses collections oriented towards new media, spanning digital pop art and installations.

INTERNATIONAL CENTER OF PHOTOGRAPHY (ICP)

79 Essex St. - ☏ 212 857 0000 - www. icp.org - daily except Mon 11am-7pm (until 9pm Thur) - $16, students and seniors $12, free under 18s; pay what you wish Thur from 5pm.

In 2020, this temple to photography, founded in 1974, moved to a brand new 40,000 square-feet home in the Lower East Side. Exhibitions dedicated to photography and visual culture fill the space, and the attached school hosts regular workshops and educational programming at all levels.

TENEMENT MUSEUM★★

103 Orchard St. - ☏ 877 975 3786 - www.tenement.org - guided tours only (leaving from Museum Shop): 10.30am-6.30pm (visiting hours vary, consult the website) - $27 - Number of visitors limited; book online.

Between 1863 and 1935, 7 000 people lived in the same **tenement building** at 97 Orchard Street. The cramped, overcrowded apartments were generally sparsely or poorly furnished. The exhibits present the homes of different families with the rooms preserved in their original state. Personal artifacts and documents tell the stories of the people who lived here: Jews fleeing Europe, clandestine Catholic Sicilian immigrants, and Irish people forced to leave by the famine.

The stories of poor and cramped living conditions, troubles and

Lower East Side Tenement Museum

© S. Raccanello/Sime/Photononstop

struggle form a moving backdrop to the exhibits. Visit the back of the visitor center and shop to watch a short film about the day-to-day life of immigrants who were often lost in a country where they barely spoke the language.

HENRY STREET

This quiet street was the heart of the first Jewish quarter. Here you will find some interesting architectural vestiges from the end of the 19C. Founded in 1893, the **Henry Street Settlement** *(no. 263)* occupied a group of renovated brick houses. It was here that Lillian Wald founded a sort of community center (the Settlement), providing poor inhabitants of the area with care, financial aid and social services. A **Settlement** took the form of a small building occupied in general by women working as nurses, teachers and social workers, helping disadvantaged people; these centers ensured the maintenance of a minimum of social integration in troubled areas. At this time, half of all Manhattan's **Settlements** could be found in the Lower East Side.

MANHATTAN BRIDGE

C8 Open to *pedestrians (south side) and cyclists (north side).*
Where LES meets Chinatown is this metal bridge linking Lower Manhattan to Dumbo (down under the Manhattan-Brooklyn overpass) in Brooklyn. Constructed in 1912, it was the fourth to be built on the East River

© Ph. Renault/hemis.fr

Manhattan Bridge seen from Dumbo

(after Brooklyn Bridge, Williamsburg Bridge and Queensboro Bridge). After an initial project proposal featuring towers crowned with minarets, which was rejected, a second design using an innovative suspension system, employing chains rather than twisted cables, was suggested, before also being rejected. The project that was finally adopted retained only the towers, with a slightly lighter aspect than those of Brooklyn Bridge.
For a fine view of the bridge and a great photo, go to Washington St on the Brooklyn side, in Dumbo *(see photo above.)*

Greenwich Village★★

Greenwich Village is known for being the spiritual home of writers, artists and dissenters and a center for jazz and blues. This was once the place of intellectuals in New York, and also the favored area of the Beat Generation and hippies. Today, it's full of celebrities, the bourgeoisie and students who attend the nearby universities. Explore the area in spring time when the white blossoms of the Japanese plum tress fall to the street and café tables spill out onto the sidewalk. Expect a bohemian atmosphere – and possibly some celebrity sightings

▶**Access:** Subway: West 4th St., Christopher St., 8th St.-NYU. Bus: M8, M11, M14A, M14D, M20, M21, M55.

***Area map p. 41**. **Detachable map AB6**.*

▶**Tip:** Visit Washington Square on the weekend to see performances by street artists. In the evening head to Bleecker Street to catch some jazz.

When New Yorkers speak about "the **Village**", they generally refer to the West – or Greenwich – Village. In 1696, the English founded the village of Greenwich. During the 18C, rich property owners lay claim to the area, but it retained its bucolic charm. The start of the 19C brought change: the establishment of 5th Avenue to the north and the development of the docks and factories along the Hudson. Bourgeois residents were replaced by new immigrants, and writers, artists and activists. At the turn of the 20C,

the Village had become a hub for the American avant-garde. Clubs and cafés served as the setting for lively meetings among political radicals, poets and painters. In 1913 **The Eight** (♿ *p. 160*) organized the Armory Show; the 1920s and 1930s were the age of New York jazz. The 1940s saw the birth of abstract expressionist painting; the 50s was the era of the Beat generation and the 60s saw the explosion of the folk music scene. The tolerant atmosphere meant that a gay community also developed

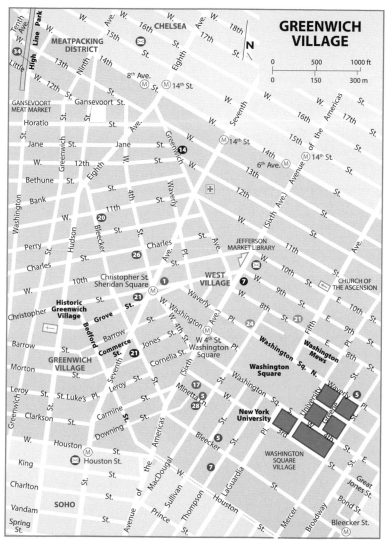

GREENWICH
VILLAGE

N

| 0 | 500 | 1000 ft |
| 0 | 150 | 300 m |

CHELSEA

MEATPACKING
DISTRICT

GANSEVOORT
MEAT MARKET

High Line Park
Tenth Ave.
Little
34

Ninth Ave.
8th Ave.
M 14th St
M

Gansevoort St.
Horatio
Jane
W. 12th St
Bethune St.
Bank
Perry
Charles
10th
W.
Christopher St

Washington
Greenwich St.
Eighth Ave.
Hudson
Bleecker

W. 16th St
W. 15th St
14th
W. 13th St

W. 14th St
Jane St.
Greenwich
Waverly
4th St.
11th
Charles St.
20
26

Eighth Ave.
W. 18th St
W. 17th St
St.
St.

Seventh Ave.
W. 16th St
W. 15th St
14th
M 14th St
13th
12th
W.

M 14th St
6th Ave. M
14
JEFFERSON
MARKET LIBRARY
11th

Avenue of the Americas
16th St
17th St
15th St
St.

Avenue (Sixth Ave.)
10th St
9th St

41

CHURCH OF
THE ASCENSION
E. 10th St
E. 9th St

WEST
VILLAGE
7

Sheridan Square
1
M
21

Historic
Greenwich
Village
Christopher
Bedford
Grove St.
Barrow
Commerce St.
27
Jones St.
Cornelia St.
Leroy

GREENWICH
VILLAGE
Morton
Leroy St.
Clarkson St.
W. Houston St.
King
Charlton
Vandam
Spring St.

Barrow
Seventh Ave.
Carmine St.
Downing

St. Luke's Pl.
Greenwich

SOHO

Waverly
W. Washington Pl.
W. 4th St.
M
Washington Ave.
24
8th St
21
Fifth Ave.

Washington Sq. N.
Washington
Mews
E. 8th St

W 4th St
Washington
Square
Cornelia St.
Minetta
17
5
28

Washington Square
New York
University

WASHINGTON
SQUARE
VILLAGE

University Pl.
Greene St.
W. 4th St.
Waverly Pl.
5
E. 8th St
Great
Jones St.
Bond St.
Bleecker St.
M

Avenue of the Americas
MacDougal
Sullivan
Thompson
LaGuardia
Houston
Bleecker
5
7
Mercer
Broadway

Prince St.

here, though not without struggle. In **Christopher Park**, you'll see statues (same-sex male and female couples) by George Segal (1924-2000). Opposite, at 53 Christopher St. is **Stonewall Inn**, the first gay bar of the area. A national monument, this is where the annual Pride parade finishes. It's famous for the violent clashes between the LGBTQ community and police that took place here in 1969, the catalyst for the LGBTQ rights movement in the US.

WASHINGTON SQUARE★

A popular spot surrounded by **New York University**, this park opens onto 5th Avenue with a Beaux-Arts style triumphal arch, finished in 1892. To the south, the impressive fountain is the backdrop for street artists. On the south side, you'll find serious players gathered round the outdoor chess boards. Over the years, Washington Square has become a place to relax, a picnic spot and a site for all manner of protest. The area around this park has always been a haunt for intellectuals. **Washington Square North**, with its elegant neo-Greek buildings, has been the address of many great writers (Henry James, Edith Wharton, John Dos Passos).

Painters Edward Hopper and Jackson Pollock, the poet Edwin Arlington Robinson and the sculptor Gertrude Vanderbilt Whitney (founder of the Whitney Museum) lived in **Washington Mews**. This little road was once the site of stables and servants' quarters. Here you'll find an idiosyncratic charm, not matched anywhere else in New York: expect whitewashed houses, climbing ivy and bucolic cobblestone.

Greenwich Village gems

At 56 7th Ave. S, you'll find **Greenwich Locksmiths**, *immediately recognizable by its amazing facade covered in keys (with a matching chair by the front door). The artwork has turned owner Philip Mortillaro into a local celebrity!*

If you watched the series Friends, you'll likely recognize the corner of Grove and Bedford Sts., which **featured as the outside shot in every episode.** *The main characters lived in Greenwich Village, but the series was actually filmed in a studio in Burbank, California. This building was chosen because it was the apartment building of one of the show's creators.*

At 17 Grove St. is a white **house with red shutters** *(1822), one of the few remaining wooden houses in the area.*

At 75 1/2 Bedford St. is another curiosity: **the narrowest house in the city,** *measuring only 2.9m /9.5ft across (and 9m /29ft deep)!*

Finally, be sure to have a peek at **Dominique Ansel Bakery,** *(189 Spring St.). Ansel invented the "cronut", a cross between a croissant and a doughnut. New Yorkers adore them and many arrive at the crack of dawn to wait in line to buy them, although now you can order at nyc.cronutpreorder.com. Only 350 are produced each day. $6 each.*

St. Luke's Place, Greenwich Village

HISTORIC GREENWICH VILLAGE★★

To the east of 6th Avenue lies the oldest part of Greenwich Village, reminiscent of what the Village would have been like at the start of the 20C, with its tree-lined roads, red brick houses and signature brownstones. On **Grove Street** are Federal-style houses, like those in verdant Grove Court *(nos. 10-12)*. The oldest, dating from 1799 stands on **Bedford Street** *(no. 77)*. At 17 Grove St., on the **northeast corner of Grove and Bedford Sts**, you'll find a three-floor wooden house, a rare sight in New York. 102 Bedford St. is also well worth a look: here you'll find

an extravagant 1925 house that looks straight out of a Bavarian village. This area is packed with significant historical sites from the world of literature and theater. On Bedford Street, watering hole **Chumley's** *(no. 86)* was frequented by the likes of Steinbeck, Willa Cather and Edna St. Vincent Millay, though note that today it's restaurant unlike the original bar. On Commerce St., **Cherry Lane Theater** *(no. 38)*, founded in the 1920s, is one of the most innovative in New York. Don't miss the quirky Twin Sisters *(nos. 39 and 41)*, two brick houses built in 1832; according to the legend, they were built by a sailor whose two daughters were incapable of living under the same roof.

© S. Amantini/Sime/Photononstop

East Village★

The East Village has quite a varied history. In the 15C, much of the area was farm. In the early 19C, handsome townhouses were built. Mid 19C saw an influx of Irish and German immigrants, then Poles and Ukrainians. In the 1950s and 60s, Beatniks, artists, musicians, and hippies moved in, followed by a strong punk and goth scene. In the 1980s, the neighborhood was the center of cool, with all-night clubs, bars, and music venues, but it was also marred by drugs, and many of the buildings were in disrepair. Today, the East Village is ultra-trendy and its real estate expensive, but its tree-lined side streets remain fairly serene.

▶**Access:** Subway: Astor Place, 1st Avenue, 2nd Avenue. Bus: M1, M2, M3, M8, M14A, M14D, M15, M102. *Detachable map C6-7*.
▶**Tip:** Pair your visit to the East Village with Greenwich Village or LES.

COOPER UNION FOUNDATION BUILDING★

C6 Built in 1859 by a self-made industrialist, this neo-Roman building is the oldest steel frame building in the city. It houses a prestigious university. In 2009, it was expanded with the curved building situated at **41 Cooper Square★**.

MERCHANT'S HOUSE MUSEUM★

BC6-7 29 East 4th St. - ✆ 212 777 1089 - www.merchantshouse.org - Thur–Mon 12pm-5pm (Thur 8pm) - tour (1hr) at 2pm - $15 (over 65s and students $10, under 12s free).
With period furnishings, this brick Federal style house shows how a rich trader and family lived in the 19C.

ST MARK'S PLACE★

C6-7 The tattoo parlors and fashionable cafés hint just lightly at this street's long-gone anarchist past.

TOMPKINS SQUARE PARK★

C7 Planted with hundred-year-old elms, this 10.5-acre (4ha) park has served as the rallying point for all manner of dissenters over the years, from socialists at the start of the 20C to Vietnam War protesters.

ST MARK'S CHURCH-IN-THE-BOWERY

C6 131 East 10th St - stmarksbowery.org. This neo-Greek style church (1799), replaced the chapel of Stuyvesant (♿ p. 150), buried in the adjoining cemetery.

RENWICK TRIANGLE★

C6 On the corner of 10th St and Stuyvesant St you'll find 16 Italian style residences in brick and sandstone, created by **James Renwick**.

Chelsea★★ and Meatpacking District★

Chelsea's main avenues are firmly 21C, but its leafy side streets, lined in red brick townhouses, are practically unchanged since the 19C. In far east Chelsea, many former warehouses have been converted into excellent free art galleries Further south, arty and sometimes snobby Meatpacking attracts slick, dressed-up New Yorkers who patronize its restaurants and clubs. Renzo Piano's sleek Whitney Museum has brought substantial culture to the area.

▶**Access:** Subway: 14th, 23rd, 28th Sts. Bus: M8, M11, M12, M14A, M14D, M20, M23
Area map p. 41. **Detachable map AB5-6**.
▶**Tip:** Start your morning with a trip to Chelsea Market, then head north, to arrive at the galleries when they open at 11am (most closed Sunday and Monday), before exploring the High Line (good for a picnic). Shoppers can opt instead to hit 6th Avenue (Avenue of the Americas), where all the big brands and a clutch of discount stores can be found. Keep the fun going into the night in the clubs of Meatpacking.

CHELSEA MARKET★

***B6** 75 9th Ave. (between 15th and 16th Sts.) - Mon-Sat 7am-9pm, Sun 8am-8pm.* Thanks to careful restoration, you can sill see the structural vestiges of the Nabisco biscuit factory (1898) that this trendy food market once was. There are many places to eat here but not a lot of seating. In nice weather, eat on the High Line or along the Hudson River.

CHELSEA HISTORIC DISTRICT★

B5 Of the old English Chelsea, there remain just a few quiet roads, lined with tall houses decked in climbing vines and wisteria. The main concentration of these can be found between 9th and 10th Avenues, along 20th, 21st and 22nd Streets. The best-preserved buildings can be found on **Cushman Row★** *(406-418 West 20th St.).* High stone staircases lead up to the red brick of the neo-Greek facades, decorated out front with matching little gardens, hemmed in by wrought iron railings.

GALLERY DISTRICT★★

B5 The largest concentration of galleries can be found to the west of 10th Avenue. Start in the south by 20th St. and head north until you

Whitney Museum of American Art, designed by Renzo Piano

Photograph by Ed Lederman/Whitney Museum of American Art

46

reach 27th St. At 529 W. 20th St., is a five-story building housing some 30 galleries. Don't be put off by the somewhat unappealing aspect of the entrance hall: the galleries of 24th St. are known for the quality of their exhibitions (visit Marianne Boesky Gallery, Luhring Augustine, Metro Pictures). The works, of varying styles, offer a fairly exhaustive cross-section of contemporary art.

RUBIN MUSEUM OF ART★★

B6 150 West 17th St. - ☎ 212 620 5000 - www.rubinmuseum.org - Thur-Mon 11am-5pm (Fri. 10pm) - $19 (over 65s and students $14, under 12s free)

Dedicated to the art of Tibet, Nepal and Bhutan (Himalaya), this museum brings together paintings, sculptures, textiles and sacred objects reflecting more than two thousand years of the cultures of these peoples. Their spirituality, approach to the world and the sophistication of their artisans are displayed elegantly in warm-toned rooms (yellow, purple). You will periodically hear incantations played, giving the experience an almost mystical dimension.

MEATPACKING DISTRICT★

B5-6 To the north of Greenwich Village is the Meatpacking district, which was the most significant center of beef production in the country in the middle of the 19C. With the development of transport, the abattoirs moved closer to the farming districts, leaving only Gansevoort Meat Market wholesale market. During the 1990s, this area had a somewhat shady reputation, but for the past two decades, its cobbled streets and vast warehouses have attracted a fashionable crowd, making this a hip district packed with cool clubs and fashion designers.

WHITNEY MUSEUM OF AMERICAN ART★★

A6 99 Gansevoort St. - ☎ 212 570 3600 - www.whitney.org - open daily 10.30am-6pm (Fri. 10pm) - closed Tues (except Jul-Aug) - $25 (seniors and students $18, pay what you wish Fri. 7-9.30pm).

The Whitney was founded in 1931 in Greenwich Village by the artist-collector Gertrude Vanderbilt Whitney. In 2015 it left its location on Museum Mile for this space, designed by Renzo Piano. The bright, modular exhibition spaces are impressive, with floor-to-ceiling windows offering views over the Hudson River and the east of Manhattan. Each floor has a beautiful terrace with a panoramic view over the High Line.

The collection centers around American art from the 20C and 21C, with a collection comprising 23000 works by more than 3000 American artists (including 3000 paintings and drawings by **Edward Hopper** alone). Only a small part of the collection is on display at any one time, with much of the space dedicated to **temporary exhibitions**, which place American art in the context of global art movements past and present.

Visitors will be taken through the beginnings of **modern American art,** with its influences from European movements—the colors of Fauvism and the geometric shapes of Cubism. Artists in the collection include Marsden Hartley, Peggy Bacon, Oscar Bluemner, Max Weber, Georgia O'Keeffe, Charles Sheeler, Stuart Davis, Arshile Gorky and Milton Avery. The collection spans the urban realism of the early 20C and more abstract geometric painting before coming to the realism of the 1930s. Though the uncontested star of the museum is Edward Hopper, you'll also find Paul Cadmus and Reginald Marsh. Next come the abstract expressionists, Robert Motherwell and Clyfford Still, Alexander Calder, and Franz Kline; contemporary artists like Andy Warhol, Kara Walker and Yayoi Kusama; and the more recent Kiki Smith.

HIGH LINE ★★

A6 www.thehighline.org

Running parallel to the Hudson, this abandoned railway line once served to transport goods for the industrialized part Manhattan's west side. The elevated section linking Gansevoort Market to 34th Street, around Chelsea and Penn Station, has been transformed into a **raised green belt**. The path starts in Meatpacking and snakes through the buildings of Chelsea and up to lower Midtown. The first section, from 14th to 20th Sts., was inaugurated in June 2009. In less than a year, it had already welcomed more than 2m visitors. The smart design facilitates a slick juxtaposition of some of the original rails with contemporary architecture, all set off by tall grasses and flowers; you'll find benches and sun loungers, great spots for watching the sun set over the Hudson in the evening.

The last section, between 30th and 34th St, opened in 2014. Along the route are several extraordinary buildings to look out for, such as the **IAC Building** (Frank Gehry), **100 11th Avenue** (Jean Nouvel) and **HL23** residence (Neil Denari). Take in the panoramic vista at the secluded viewpoint above 23rd Street.

Hudson Yards, the new face of New York

*Between 30th and 34th Sts., from the Hudson to 10th Ave, a forest of cranes announces the largest private real estate project in the history of the country. Across 1.2 million m²/12.9mft² in the heart of Manhattan, Hudson Yards will comprise a clutch of skyscrapers housing offices, hotels, apartments, shopping centers and restaurants, as well as a huge public park. The first spaces opened 2018, and the last stone of the **gargantuan building site** is expected to be placed in 2025. Hudson Yards is being framed by its developers as the new epicenter of Manhattan, and will cost around $20 billion. To attract visitors, the development is going for outrageous scale and ambition, encapsulated in two of the most unusual developments of the project. In 2020, a **suspended terrace** will open on the side of a glass skyscraper; its surface will measure 465 m2/5005ft2 and will stand 335 m/1099ft high, making it the highest observation point in the city. Opened in March 2019, **The Vessel**, a giant knot of staircases leading nowhere shaped like a bee's nest is perhaps even more astounding. This 15-storey structure contains 154 interconnected flights of stairs, 2500 steps and 80 landings.*

48 HUDSON RIVER PARK★

B4 A5-7 *www.hudsonriverpark.org*
This is another path along the Hudson. Where the High Line offers urban environs, Hudson River Park provides a different perspective: secluded from the tumult of the city.

From 59th St to **Battery Park**, you'll see cyclists, strollers, day-dreamers and joggers who come here for the protected bike and walking lanes, a cool breeze from th river, green spaces and welcoming park benches. A great spot for taking in a different, more relaxing side of New York.

Along the route, little marinas housing **cruise boats** offer trips on the Hudson and in the bay. Circle Line Cruises *(Pier 83, 42nd St at 12th Ave)* has a good reputation.

Chelsea Piers *(Pier 62 - between 17th and 23rd Sts. - ✆ 212 336 6777 - www.chelseapiers.com - ✖ - 🅿 $12/hr)* is a huge complex encompassing four piers and various sports clubs (skating, swimming, bowling, etc.) On Pier 62, children will also enjoy the pretty **carousel** on the edge of the river. Cyclists can rent **bikes** by 44th St. or use Citibike (many docks along and just opposite the path).

Union Square and Madison Square★

With Chelsea, this collection of neighborhoods links Downtown and Midtown. The west portion is home to big-name shops, public squares and beautiful cast iron buildings, including the legendary Flatiron Building. Residential areas stretch out on the east side.

▶**Access:** Subway: Union Square, 14th, 23rd, 28th Sts. ***Detachable map C6***.
▶**Tip:** Visit on Mondays, Wednesdays, Fridays and Saturdays, when the Union Square farmers' market is on.

UNION SQUARE PARK

Created in 1831, this park has long been the site of various protests, but it's also a place to sit in the shade. Around the square are some of the first skyscrapers of New York. A **farmers' market** is held here Mon., Wed., Fri., and Sat., with stalls selling dairy products, flowers, fruits and veg, and baked goods; the emphasis is on organic products,

49

Union Square Greenmarket

and all are produced in New York and the surrounding states (Pennsylvania, New Jersey, etc.). Union Square attracts aspiring artists and street musicians, as well as busy workers who stop to eat sandwiches on their lunch breaks. Bistro tables and chairs are set up on the northern side of the park, across from one of the playgrounds.

GRAMERCY PARK★

Surrounded by beautiful houses but, alas, reserved only for those who live on the park. It is one of just two private parks in New York (the other is Sunnyside Gardens in Queens).

FLATIRON BUILDING★★

This legendary building was New York's first skyscraper (1902) and, at the time, the world's highest building of its kind (87m/285ft). Its 21 floors, supported by a cast iron structure, Italian Beaux-Arts style and idiosyncratic shape are the work of **Daniel Burnham**. Its stunningly narrow iron-like shape (hence the name), occupies a triangle between Broadway, 5th Avenue and 22nd Street.

FOTOGRAFISKA NEW YORK

C6 281 Park Ave. South - www. fotografiska.com/nyc - 9am-11pm (Thur-Sat 12am) - $28 (seniors and students $18, under 12s free, free first Tues of the month from 6pm).
A Stockholm photography museum goes global with a Manhattan outpost in a historical Renaissance Revival building. Top-tier names exhibit alongside emerging talent across a breadth of themes and styles. The well-appointed restaurant and lounge make for a stunning backdrop to the culinary offerings.

THEODORE ROOSEVELT'S BIRTHPLACE

28 East 20th St. - ✆ 212 260 1616 - www.nps.gov/thrb - daily except Sun & Mon 9am-5pm - free.
The house in which the 26th US president (1901-1909) was born was constructed in 1848 and destroyed in 1916. The present-day building (1920) presents a collection of objects belonging to him and his family.

MADISON SQUARE PARK★

A lovely place to take a break. The square was once the central point of an upscale district and served as the terrain for the city's first baseball club. A few blocks away, at 4 Pennsylvania Plaza, sits the immense venue **Madison Square Garden**, site of concerts and basketball games (home of the New York Knicks).

MUSEUM OF SEX★

C5-6 233 5th Ave. - ✆212 689 6337 - www.museumofsex.com - 11am-11pm (Fri-Sat 12am), last entrance 2hrs before - $20 - under 18s not admitted.
This museum traces the history of the pornography industry in New York, from the first pin-ups of the 19C to pornographic films and magazines sex toys and erotic posters. You'll find a number of themed exhibits, some playful and funny — all of them very explicit!

Midtown West★★★ and the Theater District

Everything about Midtown is larger than life. Here, you'll find glass and steel skyscrapers, the giant neon signs of Times Square, the theaters of Broadway, the flagship stores of 5th Avenue, magical views from the Empire State Building and Rockefeller Center, and the fabulous modern and contemporary art collection at MoMA. All in all, it's enough to make you dizzy, but in the best possible way.

▶**Access:** Subway: Bryant Park, 5th Avenue, Times Sq.-42nd St, 34th St.-Herald Sq, 34th St.-Penn Station, 49th St, Rockefeller Ctr. Bus: M1, M2, M3, M4, M5, M7, M42, M55, M104.

Detachable map C4-5.

▶**Tip:** MoMA is free every Friday after 5.30pm. If you want to go to the top of the Empire State Building, allow at least 1hr for waiting in line.

BROADWAY★
THEATER DISTRICT

When New York was created, today's Midtown was just a patch of uneven countryside. But while immigration brought poor populations to the south of the city, those who made their fortune would settle further north, along 5th Avenue, followed in turn by department stores and chic hotels. This fine set needed entertaining and so the **Theater District** was born, with the opening in 1895 of the Olympia. In little time, almost 80 theaters would spring up on Broadway from 6th to 8th Avenues, between 40th and 57th Streets, around what became **Times Square★★**. Originally created for light entertainment and revues, these addresses would go on to stage the works of great American playwrights, then musicals and later erotic shows. After renovation in the 1990s, some 40 old theaters have seen a huge wave of success with the renewed popularity of Broadway musicals.

HISTORIC THEATERS

Start with **42nd Street** where you'll find the oldest, most legendary auditoriums of the Theater District, and then head north. The **New Amsterdam Theater** (1903) hosted the New York shows of Maurice Chevalier. 44th Street also has numerous auditoriums rich in history: the **Majestic** (1927), the **Shubert Theater** (1913) where Barbra Streisand played early concerts, and the **Lambs Theater** (1904). At no. 432, in a former church, you'll find the **Actors Studio** where Marlon Brando, Dustin Hoffman and Al Pacino studied, among others. On 45th Street, the **Lyceum Theater** still retains its Beaux-Arts facade (1903). The **Imperial Theater** stages famous musicals. On 46th Street, the **Lunt-Fontanne Theater** once welcomed Marlene Dietrich. On 47th Street, the **Barrymore Theater** produced *A Streetcar Named Desire* with Marlon Brando. On the corner of Broadway and 50th Street, the **Cadillac Winter Garden** was the home of the Ziegfeld

Facade, Lyceum Theater

© tupungato/iStock

Follies, who performed here with Josephine Baker.

CARNEGIE HALL

C4 *881 7th Ave. (corner of 57th St.) - ☏ 212 247 7800 - www.carnegiehall. org - guided visit 1hr (except Jul-Aug): Mon-Fri 11.30am, 12.30pm, 2pm, 3pm; Sat 11.30am and 12.30pm - tour availibility subject to Hall's schedule $19 (over 65s and students $16).*
The most famous concert hall in New York was financed by **Andrew Carnegie**, steel magnate and the son of Scottish immigrants, who was quick to become engaged with charitable works. At the end of the 19C, he decided to finance the construction of an auditorium that would be known the world over. Built in a style evocative of the Italian Renaissance, it was inaugurated on May 9, 1891, under the conducting baton of Tchaikovsky. From 1892 to 1962, this was the stage of the **New York Philharmonic Orchestra**. The interior comprises three auditoriums alternating classical, jazz and world music concerts and variety shows. The **Rose Museum** *(2nd fl. - from Sept 17-July 22: 11am-4.30pm - free)* brings together documents telling the story of more than a century's history of Carnegie Hall.

HEARST TOWER★

C4 *300 W 57th St.*
The Hearst Corporation building stands out in the city's urban landscape. The base structure, designed by architect Joseph Urban

Stockholm Syndrome

A sensational news story in the 1970s made the name Hearst famous across the world. Patty Hearst, the granddaughter of the founder of the Hearst Company, William Randolph Hearst, was kidnapped by an extreme terrorist group, the Symbionese Liberation Army, who demanded a ransom from the family. Initially treated poorly by her jailers, she developed Stockholm Syndrome, embracing the cause of her kidnappers and participating in hold-ups, for which she was jailed.

in 1928, is made of reconstituted stone, a mix of sand and concrete. Eight allegorical statues, representing comedy, tragedy, music, art, industry, sport, science and printing, are integrated into the ribbed columns. However, the 1929 stock market crash put an end to Art Deco construction. In 2006, a new tower created by Norman Foster would complete the original construction. The 40-story building features a modern glass facade, criss-crossed with superimposed steel triangles, which serve as supporting walls. In the lobby you'll find a sculpture called *Icefall*, made with thousands of glass panels, forming a waterfall that uses collected rainwater. The sculpture is embellished by a 23m/75ft fresco, *Riverlines*, created by British artist Richard Long.

TIMES SQUARE★★

C5 Crossroads of Broadway and 7th Ave. With its heaving sidewalks, bright lights and concert of car horns (at any hour, day or night), Times Square, in the heart of the Theater District, remains the **emblem** of the frenetic New York living.

In the 19C, **Longacre Square** served as a horse market. Its name changed in 1904 when the daily newspaper *The New York Times* decided to build offices here. In 1916, the installation of the first **electric signs** would be authorized, creating the now iconic look of this famous crossroads. In the golden age of movie production in New York, this district was the home of iconic studios, including Paramount and Twentieth Century Fox. In the 1970s, its reputation would diminish as a result of increasing drug dealing and the opening of sex shops in the neighboring streets. It became calmer once more in the 1990s.

Today, Times Square still contains many buildings of interest: including the HQ (until 2007) of *The New York Times*; news agency **Reuters** and the high-tech former **Condé Nast** building (Condé Nast moved to 1 WTC in 2014), recognizable by its round tower covered in screens. 2017 saw the opening of **National Geographic Encounter**, an immersive, innovative experience in the oceans of the world (though this is not an aquarium). The show is entirely based on optical illusions, 3-D imagery, and using the most up-to-date technology *(natgeoencounter.com)*.

A colossal work

The Empire State Building took only one year and 45 days to build: up to 4 000 construction workers a day worked on it, employing 60 000 tons of steel and 10 million bricks. The building has 6 500 windows, 73 ultra-fast elevators and 1 860 steps. It was meant to cost 50 million dollars, but the bill was reduced to 41 million. Its renovation, however, cost almost 100 million dollars!

MADAME TUSSAUDS WAX MUSEUM

C5 *234 42nd St. - ℘ 866 841 3505 - www.nycwax.com - June-Aug: 9am-10pm; rest of the year: 9/10am-8/10pm (depending on season) - starting at $32.* This museum displays more than 200 waxworks of celebrities, and the renderings are uncannily life-like.

54

GARMENT DISTRICT

Stretching from 30th to 40th Sts, this was for a long time the center of **dress-making and tailoring**, once one of the main industries of New York. Today workshops have moved to the Lower East Side, Chinatown and Brooklyn after rents here became prohibitively high.

The Museum at FIT – *227 West 27th St. (at 7th Ave.) - ℘ 212 217 4558 - fitnyc. edu/museum - Tue-Fri 12pm-8pm, Sat. 10am-5pm - free.* Located within the renowned fashion school, this specialized museum puts on award-winning exhibitions around different sartorial themes and fashion history.

MACY'S★

C5 *151 West 34th St. (btw Broadway and 7th Ave.) - 10am-10pm (Sun. 9pm).* Constructed in 1901, Macy's prides itself on being the largest store in the world, with 10 floors of products. Every year, the colorful **Thanksgiving Day Parade** ends here (♿ p. 146). They also have the most stunning window displays every Christmas.

5th AVENUE★★★

C5-D4 Like the theaters of Broadway, 5th Avenue, lined with chic stores, is an **emblem** of New York. This impressive urban canyon splits the city in two: from Washington Square to Harlem, all streets of Manhattan are divided by this mythic avenue into **East** or **West**. Once the setting of imposing manor houses, at the beginning of the 20C, 5th Avenue became the home of department stores and luxury boutiques. It is dotted with some of the town's finest architectural treasures and, to the west until 6th Avenue, fascinating museums, including the unmissable MoMA.

Empire State Building and the Manhattan skyline viewed from Top of the Rock

Koreatown

On W 32ᵗʰ St. (between 5ᵗʰ Ave. and Broadway) and the surrounding streets, visitors can take a trip to the Land of the Morning Calm, where businesses showcase the (sometimes unknown) mainstays of Korean cuisine and entertainment. You'll find barbecue restaurants open 24hrs and karaoke bars, popular with the businessmen of Seoul, as well as CDs from K-pop stars, DVDs of Korean films, acupuncturists, etc.

EMPIRE STATE BUILDING★★★

***C5** 350 5ᵗʰ Ave. (btw 33ʳᵈ and 34ᵗʰ Sts.) - www.esbnyc.com - 8am-2am (last elevator 1.15am) - 86ᵗʰ fl. observatory $42 (6-12 years $36, under 6s free; Main Deck Express (skip the lines) $78; Main Deck + ascent to 102ⁿᵈ fl. $72. Allow up to 2hrs for waiting in line.*
With the collapse of the twin towers of the World Trade Center, this **legendary skyscraper** once more became the **highest in the city** (443m/1453ft with the antenna) until it was overtaken by 1 World Trade Center in 2014, which measures 541m/1775ft. The Empire State Building, built in the place of the first Waldorf-Astoria hotel, was inaugurated on May 1, 1931. The whole undertaking could have easily descended into a huge fiasco, as just after the contracts were signed, the United States was plunged into the Great Depression. However, instead, its construction would act as a galvanizing force: from its beginning, the skyscraper invited awe and fantasy. In 1933, it featured in the legendary *King Kong*, with the iconic image of the giant gorilla climbing to its summit. More tragically, in 1945, as a result of foggy conditions, a plane embedded itself in the 79ᵗʰ floor, killing 14. Installed in 1953, the television antenna, surpassing the original mast, was subsequently equipped with a lantern to warn "lost" pilots. From then on, the summit of the building has been lit up every night, with colors changing depending on the occasion and season.

Observatory – Located on the 86ᵗʰ floor (320m/1050ft up), it offers one of the most beautiful panoramas★★★ of the city, showing the concrete forest of Midtown to the north and, beyond the lower buildings of Greenwich Village and Soho, the skyscrapers of southern Manhattan, including 1 World Trade Center.

NEW YORK PUBLIC LIBRARY★

***C5** 476 5ᵗʰ Ave. (btw West 40ᵗʰ and 42ⁿᵈ Sts.) - ☎ 917 275 6975 - nypl.org - Mon-Sat 10am-5.45pm (Tue-Wed 7.45pm), Sun. 1pm-4.45pm - closed bank holidays.*
The main branch of the New York Public Library (NYPL) — one of the most significant in the world — is the work of bibliophile patrons John Jacob Astor and James Lennox, generous donor Samuel Tilden, and its executor, John Bigelow. The latter

succeeded in fusing the libraries of the first two using the money of the third to construct them a unique edifice, inaugurated in 1911. Architects Carrère and Hastings were entrusted with the design; this library was one of their first Beaux-Arts style buildings. **Andrew Carnegie** would also contribute to the project. From the beautiful flight of stairs, you can admire the **colonnade** and the **pair of stone lions** that guard the entrance. If the exterior is almost intimidating in its heft, the six-level marble interior with its **spectacular glass roof** is more airy and convivial. The **collections** of books are the second largest in the country after the Library of Congress in Washington, DC.

BRYANT PARK★

C5 *Between 42nd and 40th Sts.* Backing onto the NYPL, this park is ideal for a picnic; in the summer there are concerts and films screened here. In the winter, the park turns into a winter wonderland complete with an ice rink. Look out for the buildings that border it: the impressive **American Standard Building** (1924), in black brick embellished with gold-coated terracotta, and the **HBO Building** housing the TV station.

DIAMOND DISTRICT

C5 *47th St., between 6th and 5th Aves.* 90% of diamonds that enter the US pass through this street, where the largest number of **precious stones** in the world are sold each year. Started in the south of Manhattan in the 19C,

this trade followed its rich clients northwards, towards 5th Avenue; approximately 2600 businesses established themselves here.

ROCKEFELLER CENTER★★★

C4 *5th Ave. (btw 48th and 51st Sts.) - ℘ 212 588 8601 - www.rockefeller center.com.*
At inception, Rockefeller Center was a big architectural and urban concept in New York. For the first time, a vast collection of buildings was created and unified around an idea or a style. **John D. Rockefeller Jr.**, oil magnate and the richest man in the world at the time, saw in this undertaking the opportunity to develop the area. He would base the project around the nascent radio and cinema industries. Architects would create 13 buildings around a central plaza and an emblematic skyscraper rising higher than the others around it. Works of art, a garden and open spaces allowed the public to make the space their own, transmitting the image of an ideal America. Started in 1931, finished in 1939, the initial complex was, with the exception of the World Trade Center, the most ambitious project in the city's history. In 1947 and 1973, seven new buildings were constructed. It is estimated that 65000 people worked on the site.

Rockefeller Plaza★★ – You'll arrive here from 5th Avenue along the **Channel Gardens**, between the **Maison Française** and the **British Empire Building**. This narrow walkway planted with flowers slopes down gently to the lower plaza; there's a half-buried café encircling a large terrace, lined with flags from various countries. This is where you'll find the famous ice rink, open every winter since 1936, and the gleaming statue of **Prometheus** (Paul Manship, 1934).

General Electric Building★★ – The highest skyscraper of the complex, finished in 1933 (70 floors constructed in less than 16 months), is considered a perfect example of Art Deco, both on the outside — with its straight lines and tapering floors — and within. The entrance of the plaza is decorated with colorful bas-reliefs (Lee Lawrie, 1933), centered around the theme of "Wisdom". The lobby is even more impressive, with its huge fresco by Spanish artist José Maria Sert, entitled *American Progress* (the work replaced the "offensive" creation of Diego Rivera which depicted the May Day marches led by Lenin). On the 65th floor, don't miss the superb Art Deco restaurant Rainbow Room.

Top of the Rock★★★ – **C4** - *entrance via 50th St. between 5th and 6th Aves. - 67th-70th floor - ☏ 877 692 7625 - www.topoftherocknyc.com - 8am-12am (last elevator 11.00pm) - $38 (6-12 years $28), Sun & Star ticket (two visits on the same day, one in the day and one at night, ticket valid 24h) + $10 - reserve by phone or online to choose your time.* Other than the Empire State Building, this is the way to get a bird's eye view of Manhattan. From the terrace (259m/850ft), you can admire the Empire State Building and Central Park. The magnificent

atrium★★★, spanning three glass-lined floors, presents the history of Rockefeller Center. The long, narrow observatory, reminiscent of the deck of a boat, offers a fantastic **panorama★★★** over Midtown: go at night to fully appreciate the city lights.

NBC STUDIO TOUR★

C4 *30 Rockefeller Plaza - ☏ 212 664 3700 - www.nbcstudiotour.com - 8.20am-2.20pm on weekdays, until 5pm on the weekend (departs every 20mins) - $33 (6-12 years $29).*
On this studio visit, you'll discover the history of station NBC, spanning the beginnings of radio and the transition to television.

RADIO CITY MUSIC HALL★

C4 *1260 6th Ave. (corner of 50th St.).*
A typical example of Art Deco architecture, this music hall (1932), the largest covered theater in the world, was part of the larger complex of Rockefeller Center. Traditionally film premieres were held here. It now welcomes musical shows, of which the most popular is the *Radio City Christmas Spectacular.*

MUSEUM OF MODERN ART (MOMA)★★★

C4 *11 West 53rd St. (between 5th and 6th Aves) - ☏ 212 708 9400 - www. moma.org - daily 10am-5.30pm (Fri. and first Thur. of each month 9pm) - closed 25 Dec and Thanksgiving - $25 (students $14, under 16s free), free Fri*

5.30pm-9pm; ticket includes entry to PS1. (♿ p. 99) - map and audio guide included w/ticket - children's audio guide available. Allow between 1hr30min to 3hrs.

Its light interior architecture, sculpture garden and incredible collection of masterpieces make a visit to **MoMA** a fascinating journey through the art of the 19C to the present. It was founded in 1929 by three women: **Abby Rockefeller** (whose husband created Rockefeller Center), **Lillie Bliss** and **Mary Sullivan**, who wished to create a space for modern art. The museum has gone through several major renovations and expansions. Most recently, in 2019, MoMA underwent a $450 million expansion, resulting in additional galleries and performance spaces, a new first-floor gallery focused on contempoary design, and a revamped bookstore. MoMA is arranged around a spectacular lobby. Take in the views out over the **Sculpture Garden★★**, which is dotted with benches and open to visitors (weather permitting).

Paintings and sculptures★★★ occupy the 4th and 5th floors *(allow 1hr30min to 2hr)*. The works do not follow a strictly chronological order and are not grouped by artist. Instead, they are grouped thematically, with the idea of showing how different artists or artistic movements can be linked, even if they are from very different eras.

The **Impressionists** are represented by Pierre Bonnard, Édouard Vuillard and Claude Monet including the triptych *Reflections of the Clouds on the Water Lily Pond* (1920), which occupies an entire room.

The **Post-Impressionists** moved towards pared-down lines and more stark colors. Among them, Georges Seurat (*Evening, Honfleur*, 1886), Paul Cézanne (*The Bather,* 1885), Paul Gauguin and Henri Rousseau. Vincent Van Gogh is celebrated with *The Olive Trees* (1889) and the famous *Starry Night* (1889).

The **Fauves**, taking in André Derain and the first works of Matisse, are identifiable by their bold rush strokes and panels of color. After this movement, Picasso developed a new painting style. His early canvasses help track his long evolution, from the soft colors and figurative models of his nudes from the Rose Period to the *Demoiselles d'Avignon* (1907), where we trace the influence of Oceanic art and the move towards **Cubism**. This is underlined in works such as *Boy leading a Horse* (1905-1906), *Woman with Pears* (1909) and *Ma Jolie* (1911-1912). It is in comparing Picasso and Georges Braque that we really begin to approach Cubism. The museum's collection contains work from Juan Gris and many pieces by Henri Matisse, including Matisse's famous *Dance*. Next, there are more Picassos, various works from Giorgio de Chirico and Fernand Léger and Brancusi sculptures.

Expressionism is characterized by depictions distorted by the emotions of the artist. Shapes are stylized and colors often bold. German artists were at the forefront of this movement, represented in the MoMA collection by paintings from Oskar Kokoschka, Paul Klee and Vassily Kandinsky (*Picture with an Archer,* 1909).

The first **abstract art** followed naturally from Cubism, but the geometric shapes and large colored surfaces were no longer used to emulate th find Marc Chagall, Robert Delaunay, Kazimir Malevich and Fernand Léger. In another style, the Mondrian room introduces a purely plastic form of this art.

The **Dada movement** and **surrealism** also occupy a vast room, which includes collages from Picasso and Braque. You'll find the montages of Francis Picabia, Marcel Duchamp and Kurt Schwitters. Among the great surrealists, you can admire André Breton, Joan Miró with *Hirondelle Amour* (1933), Max Ernst, René Magritte and Salvador Dalí (*The Persistence of Memory,* 1931). In terms of sculptures, there are some remarkable statues in the style of **primitive deities** from Giacometti. There is no shortage, either, of the **American painters**, with a collection spanning Edward Hopper and Charles Sheeler.

On the 4th floor, other great names of American painting are brought together with **abstract expressionism**, from the middle of the 20C to today: Helen Frankenthaler, Jackson Pollock, Willem De Kooning with *Woman I* (1950), Mark Rothko, Clyfford Still, Robert Motherwell, Robert Rauschenberg and Jasper Johns, but also English artist Francis Bacon.

Beside Andy Warhol and *Gold Marilyn Monroe* (1962), you'll find **pop art** spanning James Rosenquist, Claes Oldenburg and Roy Lichtenstein.

A wing dedicated to **design★★** covers both the progress of technology in everyday objects and the development of aesthetics during the 20C, from the cooking utensils of the 1930s and 1940s to the very first computers, taking in humble and more extravagant furniture.

The **photography** department traces the history of this medium from the middle of the 19C and its journalistic, artistic and commercial applications. The collection of **drawings★** presents works in pencil, ink and charcoal, as well as collages and watercolors.

INTREPID SEA, AIR & SPACE MUSEUM★

B4 Pier 86 (at 46th St. and 12th Ave.) - ℘ 212 245 0072 - www.intrepid museum.org - 10am-5pm (Sat-Sun and public holidays from April to October 6pm) - $33 ticket (Above 65s $31, 5-12 years $24).

This open-air museum brings together boats from the US Navy, including the *Intrepid* —an aircraft carrier from the Second World War, also used during the Vietnam War and the Cuban Missile Crisis. You'll also find a collection of planes, including *Concorde,* as well as the *Enterprise*, **NASA's first space shuttle** (in the Space Shuttle Pavilion).

Midtown East ★

The eastern part of Midtown developed at the same time as its neighbor to the west, but the focus here is business rather than theater. With the presence of Grand Central station, this area became a center for trade, and the construction of office buildings inevitably followed. The proximity to 5th Avenue attracted luxury hotels and prestigious institutions, such as The Morgan Library and the headquarters of the United Nations.

▶**Access:** 33rd St, Grand Central-42nd St, 51st St. Bus: M15, 34, M42, M50
Detachable map CD5.
▶**Tip:** For great photos of the Chrysler Building, use a telephoto lens and head to 3rd Avenue, between 42nd and 44th Streets. Bring binoculars to fully admire the detail of its architecture.

MURRAY HILL★

C5 Located between 30th and 40th Sts, the south part of Midtown East owes its name to Robert Murray, a merchant of English origin who would construct his "country house" here. For some time this was a quiet, leafy area occupied by bourgeois houses and the stables of the palaces of 5th Avenue. Today, the manor houses have been replaced by department stores, and the stables by residential buildings.

MORGAN LIBRARY★★

C5 *225 Madison Ave. - ℘ 212 685 0008 - www.themorgan.org - Tue-Thur 10.30am-5pm, Fri 10.30am-9pm, Sat 10am-6pm, Sun 11am-6pm - closed Mon, 1 Jan, Thanksgiving and 25 Dec - $22 (over 65s $14, students $13, under 12s free); free Friday from 7pm to 9pm. Allow between 1hr and 1hr30min.*

In the 19C, one of the richest men in New York, **John Pierpont Morgan** (1837-1913), built a luxurious Neoclassical-style residence in Murray Hill. In 1924, his son granted his father's wish to turn the family's private collections (of antique printed books and rare manuscripts) into a public institution. Since this time, it has been added to with donations and acquisitions. The current renovated premises bring together the homes of the father and son. The collections of **manuscripts**, **sheet music** and **literature** are impressive, spanning scores from Mozart, Beethoven, Brahms, Chopin, Verdi and others, without forgetting the modern Schoenberg and Cage; literary manuscripts, letters and notes from Galilei, Milton, Poe, Byron, Charles Dickens, Mark Twain, Thoreau, Oscar Wilde, John Steinbeck, Ernest Hemingway, and Jane Austen, while one of the three remaining editions of the Gutenberg Bible is painstakingly conserved in the majestic East Room. You will also find intricate bookbindings encrusted with precious gemstones and rare manuscripts, of which the oldest dates from the 7C. Sacred objects and paintings are kept in Morgan's office: Perugino's *Madonna, Portrait of a Man* by *Tintoretto, Portraits of Martin Luther and his wife* by Lucas Cranach the Elder, as well as a number of drawings by Michelangelo, da Vinci, Dürer, Rembrandt, Watteau, Goya, Ingres, Degas and Van Gogh.

GRAND CENTRAL TERMINAL★★

C5 *Corner of Park Ave. South and 42nd St - www.grandcentralterminal. com - 5.30am-2am - folding guide available in the central kiosk - audio guide with map $12 (over 65s $10, students $11) at counters marked GCT Tour (daily 9am-6pm); guided tour (1hr15min, $30, over 65s and students $20) daily at 12.30pm organized by the Municipal Art Society of New York.* In 1871, railway magnate, **Cornelius Vanderbilt** constructed a first station, which was replaced by the current edifice in 1913. On the ground site of the old station, Park Avenue and Madison Avenue were created. In the place of buildings black with soot, residences and chic hotels were built, and later skyscrapers, giving the area a fine variety of 20C architecture. With its horizontal access to the platforms, which could also be reached directly from the subway, the layout of the **station** was revolutionary at the time. In 1947,

© Graham Haber/The Morgan Library & Museum

Pierpont Morgan's Library,
The Morgan Library & Museum

it was estimated that 65 million passengers swarmed through here each year; today more than 75000 pass through daily. Landmarked in 1978 and superbly renovated in 1998, it is now a hub for regional trains. Its impressive Beaux-Arts facade is adorned with a clock surrounded by Mercury, Minerva and Hercules. The **Main Concourse**, 12 stories high, is topped with a painted and electrified **vault** depicting the constellations (represented backwards; the west is found in the east!). Imposing staircases lead up to balconies. The glimmering little central kiosk is one of the mythical meeting points of the city.

63

CHRYSLER BUILDING★★★

D5 *Corner of 42nd St. and Lexington Ave.*

This may not be the tallest skyscraper in New York, but it is incontestably the most beautiful: its finesse and refined elegance and its delicate spire are unparalleled. Built in 1930 at the behest of the car maker **Walter Chrysler**, the Chrysler Building was born of the imagination of architect **William Van Alen** who wanted to construct the tallest building in the world (319m/1046ft, 77 stories). It did not hold the record for long, as it was overtaken the following year by the Empire State Building. Its originality lies in the use of steel as an embellishment, emphasizing the play of light on its structure and accentuating its soaring silhouette. It is one of the most spectacular examples of Art Deco architecture, featuring niches, gargoyles in the shape of eagles' heads (in a nod to the Chrysler hood ornaments), alternating curved and triangular lines and a summit evoking the chrome detailing of the automobile. On the inside, the lobby is just as impressive, featuring red marble, geometrical friezes, the eagle motif and a fresco on the ceiling exploring the theme of transport and industry.

UNITED NATIONS HEADQUARTERS (UN) ★★

D5 *On the edge of the East River, btw 42nd and 48th Sts., visitors' entrance 46th St. and 1st Ave. - ✆ 212 963 8687 - www.visit.un.org -guided tours only (1hr): Mon-Fri 9am-4.30pm (arrive 1hr before the beginning of the tour for security checks, ID required) - closed public holidays - children under 5 not allowed - $22 (over 60s and students $15, 5-12 years $12), online reservation only.*

Created on October 24, 1945, the UN is an intergovernmental community tasked with maintaining peace in the world. The decision to create the headquarters in New York was taken at the first General Assembly in 1946. The land dedicated to the project, bought thanks to a donation from John D. Rockefeller Jr., benefits from a special status placing it outside of American jurisdiction.

The visitor enters the complex via an esplanade decorated with two symbolic sculptures: *Non-Violence*, the revolver with a knotted barrel (Carl Fredrik Reuterswärd, 1988), and *Sphere Within Sphere* (Arnaldo Pomodoro, 1996). On the right, the **General Assembly Building** (1952), with its curved facade houses the United Nations General Assembly, where the delegates of member states meet. Set back on the riverside, we find the **Conference Building**, which houses conference and meeting rooms. This is the home of, among other functions, the

Chrysler Building

Security Council, composed of fifteen member states, of which only five are permanent (the US, China, Russia, France and the UK). The most famous building is the blue-gray glass skyscraper that dominates the complex: the **Secretariat Building** (1950). It houses, as its name suggests, the offices of the Secretary General and all their services.

TUDOR CITY★

D5 Created for middle-class residents by promoter Fred F. French, the idea of the complex was to create a town within a town, with 3000 apartments, a hotel, shops and green spaces. The 12 brick buildings are decorated with flower-adorned apexes in flamboyant Gothic style, evoking English Tudor style.
Odd fact: The buildings on the east side only have a few windows because, at the time of their construction, the contemporary site of the esplanade of the United Nations was an industrialized area. From **Tudor City Place**, take the alley that crosses 42nd Street *(access via steps from 42nd and 43rd Sts.)* to discover a superb **view★**.

SAINT PATRICK'S CATHEDRAL★★

CD5 *5th Ave., between 50th and 51st Sts. - www.saintpatrickscathedral.org - 6am-8pm - guided tours 9am-5pm (see website for details).*
Enclosed between the surrounding high buildings, one of the first grand neo-Gothic churches in America seems strangely small, though its towers actually stretch to over 100m/328ft.
Inspired by Cologne Cathedral, it was conceived by architect **James Renwick Jr.** in 1879. Opposite the edifice stands the bronze statue of **Atlas** carrying the world on his shoulders (Lee Lawrie, 1937).

PALEY PARK★ AND GREENACRE PARK★

D5 *Leave 5th Ave. heading east: Paley Park is on East 53rd St. between 5th Ave. and Madison Ave.; Greenacre Park is on 51st St. btw 3rd and 2nd Aves.* These pockets parks provide a brief escape from the hubbub of the Big Apple.
A place for meditation and relaxation, **Greenacre Park** is frequented by tourists as well as city workers savoring their lunch breaks. Take a seat on a chair dotted amid the flowers and trees, and take in the relaxing soundtrack of birdsong and the running water of an artificial waterfall, all hemmed in by walls of climbing ivy.
Closer to 5th Ave, and offering a little less charm than Greenacre Park despite a number of the same features (wall of water, tables and chairs, flowerbeds), **Paley Park** is principally known for its fragments of the Berlin Wall.

Central Park★★★

Gone are the lines of honking taxis, the graffiti, the never-ending thrum of traffic: Central Park is a green haven, a sprawling countryside in the heart of the city. All around, the skyscrapers seem almost modest, despite their sophisticated silhouettes. Under the park's huge trees, the city is almost forgotten, and yet, New York is just there.

▶**Access:** Subway: A, B, C, and D trains run up the west side; 4, 5, and 6 run up the east side. Bus: M66, M72, M79, M86, M96 and M106 cross Central Park. *Detachable map C-D4, D3, E2.*

▶**Tip:** You can start at the southern end of the park and leave at the top (or vice versa) while visiting **Museum Mile★★★** (♿ *p. 70*) on the way. Be sure to get the full experience by stopping for a picnic. There is a supermarket at Columbus Circle and many along the avenues on the east and west side.

Central Park (www.centralparknyc.org) has 93 km/57mi of paths. Maps, event calendars and timetables available in the three welcome centers of the park (The Dairy in the center of the park, Dana Discovery Center in the north and Belvedere Castle). Tours available.

In the 18C, the north of Manhattan was the site of farms and summer residences of a few wealthy individuals. With the rise of urbanization, the bourgeois decided to live in their manor houses year-round. The central part of this zone was left as foul-smelling marshland, dotted with giant rocks, squatted on by a contingent of poor and marginalized New-Yorkers. **William Cullen Bryant** (for whom Bryant Park is named), a literary man and editor of the *New York Evening Post*, launched in 1850 a powerful press campaign with the aim of creating a park comparable to the great European green spaces.

Central Park was finished in 1873, 16 years after ground was broken. It was the work of architects and landscapers **Frederick Olmsted** and **Calvert Vaux,** who envisaged the park as a series of living tableaux presenting an ideal of nature. The project required 20 000 workers, planting half a million trees and millions of feet of earth, imported by boat, which would fill the swamps and the space left by the destruction of 300 000 t of rocks. In the end the Park cost the United States double the Alaska Purchase ($7.4m vs. 7.2m)! With its 341ha/842 acres, Central Park is the **green lungs of New York**. Visitors come for respite from the city, but without really leaving it thanks to the surrounding crown of skyscrapers. In terms of cultural events and public celebrations, it's a major site, at the heart of all big city events. New Yorkers spontaneously gather here in times of trouble, as happened after the September 11th attacks, or at times of dissent, against war or in favor of a humanitarian cause. After a low period that ended in the 1980s, during which parts of the park were considered unsafe, the park re-established itself as a place for families, nature-lovers, sporty types and tourists. 20 million people come to this park every year.

CENTRAL PARK ZOO

D4 centralparkzoo.com Apr-Oct: 10am-5pm (Sat-Sun and public holidays 5.30pm); rest of the year: 10am-4.30pm - $20 (3-12 years $15). Above the entrance arch chimes the **Delacorte Clock** and its animated animal figurines. More than 450 animals are in this zoo, separated into three key climates (temperate, tropical and polar). The children's zoo has the only cow in Manhattan.

BETHESDA FOUNTAIN TERRACE★

D3-4 **The Mall** is a majestic alley set in the shadow of gigantic elm trees. It's overlooked in the south by a statue of Shakespeare. On its left spreads the prairie of **Sheep Meadow**, where picnickers and Frisbee throwers have replaced the sheep (the old sheep pen, to the west, has been converted into restaurant Tavern on the Green). The mall leads to **Bethesda Fountain Terrace★**, an elegant esplanade and one-time meeting point for hippies during the counter-culture movement of the 20C. Considered

the master feature of the park, this pretty sandstone terrace resembles a Spanish patio with its stairs and central statue-adorned fountain.

THE LAKE★★

D3 The Bethesda Fountain Terrace sits next to the Lake of which the irregular form is dominated by the craggy hill of the **Ramble**, criss-crossed with paths. To the west, the **Strawberry Fields** memorial garden takes its name from the song penned by John Lennon, who was assassinated at the foot of the Dakota Building, just by this point of the park. Bypassing the lake on the right, you arrive at **Loeb Boathouse**, where you can rent row boats, get something to eat or stop for a drink. You can cross the lake via the elegant metal **Bow Bridge★★**, stepping out onto the north side.

JACQUELINE KENNEDY ONASSIS RESERVOIR★

DE3 Farther to the north you'll find the Jacqueline Kennedy Onassis Reservoir, a legendary spot for joggers (Dustin Hoffman runs round it in *Marathon Man*). As you pass behind the Metropolitan Museum, note **Cleopatra's Needle**, an obelisk of which the (translated) hieroglyphics tell the story of Thutmose III (15C BC). It was given to the city of New York by the Khedive of Egypt, Isma'il Pasha (transported to the United States in 1880).

Central Park in autumn

Upper East Side★★★ *and Museum Mile*★★★

This is one of the most expensive neighborhoods in Manhattan. 5th Avenue is bursting with prestigious apartment blocks. In front of these elegant residences, you'll see door staff standing to attention, ready to welcome the moneyed residents home from their outings—a shopping trip, perhaps. All around you'll find museums housed in imposing manor houses, displaying the area's affinity to culture, as well as the generosity of wealthy patrons.

▶**Access:** Subway: lines 4, 5 and 6 between 63rd and 110th Sts and the Q at 72nd, 86th, and 96th Sts. Bus: M1 to 4, M66, M72, M79, M86, M96, M98, M101 to 103.

Detachable map DE4, DF3, E2.

▶**Tip:** The Guggenheim is pay what you wish Saturday evenings; Cooper Hewitt on Tuesday evenings; and the Frick on Wednesdays 2-6pm. Expect a long line at the Guggenheim.

MUSEUM MILE★★★

This name refers to the section of 5th Avenue that runs alongside Central Park. Here, billionaires built the most splendid manor houses of the city, and then at the start of the 20C made donations to create foundations. As a result, this short section of avenue hosts a heavy concentration of some of the world's most beautiful museums, as well as the most exclusive private mansions in New York — in Beaux-Arts or Queen Anne style — adorned with opulent awnings. Starting from **Grand Army Plaza** (not to be confused with the one in Brooklyn), dominated by the **Pulitzer Fountain** (1915) and

the equestrian statue of General Sherman (1903), you can see the **General Motors Building**, the **Plaza** (1907) and The Pierre hotel, which welcomes the international jet-set. The prestigious Knickerbocker Club (1870, *no. 810*) is reserved for the descendants of the Dutch pioneers. The Beaux-Arts style **Marshall Orme Wilson House** (1903, *3 E. 64th St.*) is now the Indian consulate. **Harkness House** (1900, 1 E. *75th St.*), set in an Italian Renaissance-style mansion, is the home of the Commonwealth Fund, a philanthropic association. James B. Duke House (*1 E. 78th St.*), a Neoclassical edifice inspired by a Louis XVI-style Bordeaux château, is the setting of the **New York Institute** of Fine Arts. The cultural and press services of the French consulate are housed in the Beaux-Arts style former residence (1906, *972 5th Ave.*) of Payne Whitney. The **Ukrainian Institute of America**, in a stunning little château in French Renaissance style (1897, *2 E. 79th St.*), is housed in the residence of the Stuyvesants, descendants of New York's first governor. The former **Goethe House** (1957, *1014 5th Ave.*) is a Beaux-Arts style residence.

TEMPLE EMANU-EL★

D4 1 East 65th St. - ℘ 212 744 1400 - *www.emanuelnyc.org - Sun-Thur 10am-4pm - no visiting on Jewish holidays.*
With a capacity of 2500 worshippers, this Roman-Moorish-Byzantine style synagogue (1929) is one of the largest in the world. Its majestic nave is covered in oriental motif mosaics. A sacred arch encloses the scrolls of the Torah. A small **museum** houses a collection of liturgical objects and hosts temporary exhibitions.

THE FRICK COLLECTION★★★

D4 1 East 70th St. - ℘ 212 288 0700 - *www.frick.org - Tue-Sat 10am-6pm, Sun 11am-5pm - closed public holidays - $22 (over 65s $17, students $12); free Wed. 2-6pm and first Fri. of every month 6-9pm - audio guide included in the ticket - an introductory film (11min) is projected every 20min in the music room - under 10s not permitted. Allow 2-3hrs.*
As of this writing, The Frick is planning to renovate. Check web for updated

hours, admission, and map and see frickfuture.org for more details.
This delectable little museum is an ideal initiation to classical painting. Millionaire steel magnate **Henry Frick** (1849-1919) asked architects Carrère and Hastings to build him a prestigious manor house in Neoclassical style close to Central Park (1913). An art enthusiast, he would exhibit part of his magnificent collection here, which he acquired in Europe. On his death, he bequeathed his residence and the artwork to an administrative council, who would turn them into a museum in 1935. The **Boucher Room** and the **Anteroom** recreate an 18C boudoir, decorated with tableaux by François Boucher (1752). The furnishings comprise a Riesener mahogany flat desk (18C), Sèvres porcelain pieces and an Indian rug (16C). In the antechamber hangs the oldest portrait by Hans Memling. The **Dining Room** is decorated with English paintings by Hogarth, Romney, Reynolds Gainsborough and James Park. The **West Vestibule** presents *The Four Seasons* by Boucher (1775) as well as a bureau by Charles Boulle. Eleven canvases by Fragonard *(The Progress of Love)* are conserved in the **Fragonard Room**, accompanied by magnificent furnishings from the School of Paris, Sèvres porcelain and a marble bust of the Countess of Cayla, by Houdon. The **South Hall** exhibits three of Vermeer's 37 known canvases : *Officer and Laughing Girl* (around 1658), *Girl Interrupted at Her Music* (around 1660) and *Mistress and Maid* (around 1666). The **Living Hall**

71

is filled with major works: *Saint Francis* by Bellini, *Portrait of a Man in a Red Cap* by Titian, two portraits by Holbein the Younger and *Saint Jerome* by El Greco. Some fine smaller paintings from the English school are presented in the **Library**.

In the **North Hall** you'll find the famous portrait *The Countess of Haussonville* by Ingres, *The Portal of Valenciennes* by Watteau, a Degas, a Monet and a Houdon bust. The largest room in the museum, the **West Gallery**, decorated with Italian furniture from the 16C, is adorned with works from the Italian, Dutch, Spanish, English and French schools: Bronzino, Véronèse, Van Dyck, Hobbema, Van Ruysdael, Frans Hals, de La Tour, El Greco, Rembrandt, Goya, Vélasquez and Turner. Visitors can admire a collection of painted enamels from the Limoges school of the 16 and 17C, as well as Italian primitives and Renaissance in the **Enamel Room**. The **Oval Room** is the setting of a rare terracotta replica of *Diana the Huntress* by Houdon. The **East Gallery** brings together exquisite works from Claude Lorrain, Greuze, Goya, Gainsborough, Van Dyck and Van Ruysdael. In the **Garden Court**, you can admire Manet's *The Bullfight* and a Whistler seascape.

MET BREUER★★

D4 Ⓜ 6 (station 77ᵗʰ St.). Bus M1-4, M101-M103. 945 Madison Ave. (at 75ᵗʰ St.) - ℘ 212 731 1675 - www. metmuseum.org/visit/met-breuer - Tue-Sun 10am-5.30pm (Fri-Sat 9pm)

- $25 (seniors $17, students $12), ticket valid for 3 consecutive days at The Cloisters (Ⓓ p. 94) and The Met (Ⓓ p. 74).

When the Whitney Museum moved to Meatpacking (Ⓓ p. 45), the Met set up home in its concrete and granite building, created in 1966 by Hungarian architect Marcel Breuer. Thanks to the billionaire Leonard Lauder, son of cosmetics giant Estée Lauder, the Met was able to enrich its offer of contemporary and modern art (which was really lacking up to this point) and today competes with the Whitney, the Museum of Modern Art (MoMA) and the Guggenheim, which themselves have significant collections. Playing with time periods, the Met Breuer presents **themed exhibitions** where the classic masters (Rembrandt, Turner and Cézanne) are blended with essential figures of modern and contemporary art (Jackson Pollock, Picasso and Robert Rauschenberg).

ASIA SOCIETY AND MUSEUM★★

D4 725 Park Ave. (corner of 70ᵗʰ St.) - ℘ 212 288 6400 - asiasociety.org/ museum - Tue-Sun 11am-6pm (Fri 9pm Sep-June) - closed public holidays - $12 (under 16s free); free Fri. 6-9pm (except Jul-Aug) - audio guide included.

Founded by **John D. Rockefeller III** (1956), this space is both a museum and a cultural center exploring art and design, but also the relationship between West and East. The superbly curated **collections★★** span the whole Indian subcontinent, the Himalayas,

Fragonard Room The Frick Collection

Southeast Asia, China, Korea and Japan. The building's **architecture★** is remarkable with its steel and blue glass **staircase** linking the levels.

METROPOLITAN MUSEUM OF ART (MET)★★★

D3 1000 5th Ave. (at 82nd St.) - Ⓜ lines 4, 5 and 6 (station 86th Street). Bus lines 1, 2, 3 and 4 (station 82nd Street) - ☏ 212 535 7710 - www.metmuseum. org - 10am-5.30pm (Fri-Sat 9pm) - closed Jan 1, Thanksgiving, Dec 25 and first Monday in May - $25 (seniors $17, students $12), ticket valid for 3 consecutive days at The Cloisters (♿ p. 94) and The Met Breuer (♿ p. 72); audio guide $7 - guided tour included in the price of the ticket - Allow 2-4hrs.

This legendary museum, one of the four or five leaders of its kind in the world, stretches in grand style off 5th Avenue, framed by heavy columns and surrounded by Central Park. Its carefully curated collections span Sumerian antiquities to the art of the 20C. The museum, which owes its existence to a number of bequests and donations from rich patrons, was created in 1870. Its Beaux-Arts facade dates from 1902, but the north and south wings are from 1911 and 1913 respectively. Other structural additions followed, such as the Lehman Pavilion (1975), the Sackler Wing (1978), the Petrie Court (1990), the Greek and Roman rooms (2007) and the section dedicated to Oceanic art.

Greek and Roman antiquities★★

First floor (ground floor), rooms 150-172, and second floor (first floor), rooms 173-176. These rooms present the roots of Western art, from Greek prehistory to the end of the Roman Empire. The history of Greek art is traced from the **Geometric Period** (8C BCE) to the **Hellenistic period** (3rd-2ndC BCE), taking in the **Archaic** and **Classical** period. Roman civilization is also well represented with the sophisticated reconstruction of a bedroom from the era, adorned with superb frescoes (1C BCE.). Don't miss the vestiges of the **Etruscan civilization**. On the first floor, there is a gallery dedicated to **Cypriot art** with the stunning *Amathus sarcophagus* (5C BCE).

Art of Africa, the Americas and Oceania ★★★

First floor *(ground floor), rooms 350-359.* **Nelson Rockefeller** made a donation of part of his collection in memory of his son Michael, who disappeared in 1961 on an expedition in New Guinea.

Art of Africa – More or less every facet of the ritual art of the major African tribes are presented here. Masks and statues constitute the biggest part of the collection, with some rarities, such as a sitting statuette, *Seated Figure* (Mali, 13C), a poignant evocation of the desolation of grief. The Dogon masks are particularly beautiful, as are the Benin bronzes.

Art of the Americas – The furniture exhibited evokes diverse civilizations from Mexico, Peru, Colombia

and Ecuador. Don't miss the **Jan Mitchell Treasury**, an incredible series of pre-Columbian gold (from 1-16C.). The sumptuous ceremonial knives in gold and turquoise, the death masks, such as the mask of Sícán (Peru, 1011C), the beaten gold cups, the figurines and jewelry are all fascinating.

Arts of Oceania – The more pared down Oceanic statuettes undoubtedly inspired the silhouettes painted by Matisse and Picasso. Note the fly whisks in ivory and whale bone of Tahitian king Pomare II (18C). Among the masks, those from the Solomon Islands and Vanuatu are particularly spectacular. The collection of ritual objects from Papua New Guinea exhibits a striking sobriety.

Modern art★★★

First (rooms 900-926) and second (rooms 917-925) floors, mezzanine. American painting of the 20C is represented by linchpins Edward Hopper, Georgia O'Keeffe, Stuart Davis, Charles Sheeler, Arthur Dove and Marsden Hartley. The international modern art collection centers around major figures such as Picasso (Seated Harlequin, 1901), The Actor (1904-1905), Cavalier and Seated Nude (1967). Admire Matisse and his Young Sailor (1906), Balthus and The Mountain (1937) and the paintings and statuettes of Giacometti. You can discover the first works of Joan Miró, Dubuffet and his View of Paris with Furtive Pedestrians (1944), as well as Yves Tanguy, Max Ernst and Dalí. Don't miss the delightful Bonnards (Après

la toilette du matin, 1910) and the colorful canvases of Derain (The Sunken Path, L'Estaque, 1906). Among the other famous pieces, stop to contemplate Jeanne Hébuterne (1919) by Modigliani, the Paul Klees, including Redgreen and Violet-Yellow Rhythms (1920). Next you will come to the most famous Americans of the 20C: Louise Bourgeois, Clyfford Still, Rothko, Franz Kline, Willem De Kooning (Woman, 1944), Jackson Pollock and the stars of pop art, Andy Warhol and Roy Lichtenstein. The roof terrace hosts monumental sculpture exhibitions.

Decorative arts and European sculpture★★

First floor (ground floor), rooms 500-556. The period covered by the **sculptures** goes from the Renaissance to the start of the 20C. Highlights include Houdon, Rodin and several Italian sculptors. The **decorative arts** collection takes in furniture, ceramics, textiles, painting, fine gold and silver work and glassware. Reconstructions of rooms give an idea of the successive style trends of England and France in particular.

Medieval art★★★

First floor (ground floor), rooms 300-307. This enormous collection, organized around a central hall, brings together more than 4000 works of art, from the fall of the Roman Empire to the Renaissance. It spans the major waves of medieval art, from Byzantium and its influence on the Flemish, English, Italian and French styles.

© T. Abad/age fotostock

Metropolitan Museum of Art, 5th Avenue

Among the remarkable pieces, it is worth drawing attention to the stunning rosary beads★★ in ivory or wood sculpted from delicate religious scenes, the **cut-away enamel cases★★★** (Limoges, 12C-13C),the exceptional altarpiece★★★ in bone and ivory recounting the lives of Jesus, John the Baptist and John the Evangelist (Northern Italy, 1390-1400), as well as the painted altarpieces of the 15C and 16C. Among the collections of sacred treasures, you'll also find spectacular objects such as a series of reliquaries★★ as well as processional crosses and objects of worship.

The Robert Lehman Collection★★

First floor *(ground floor), rooms 950-965*. The collections of this banker and his son—taking in furniture, painting and sculpture—are displayed in rooms resembling those of the home of the donors. Here you'll find Italian Primitives, including a superb *Nativity* (1409) by Lorenzo Monaco and an *Annunciation* (1485) by Botticelli; Dutch painters, with an *Annunciation* by Hans Memling; and some French impressionists, including the *Two Young Girls at the Piano* (1892) by Renoir. Note also the *Nude in Front of a Mantel* (1955) by Balthus.

American Wing★★★

First *(rooms 700-774) and* second *(703-772)* floors, *mezzanine.* Only American painters born before 1876 (with the exception of The Eight) are exhibited here, with the others housed with modern art (⟵ p. 74).

American decorative arts – A series of reconstructions of furnished rooms chart the evolution of styles and European influences throughout the 19C. (William and Mary style, Queen Anne style, Chippendale style, the Arts and Crafts movement). The typically American **Prairie School** is illustrated by the famous Francis W. Little House (Wayzata, Minnesota, 1912-1914), of which we can see the living room, decorated by Frank Lloyd Wright. Make a stop at **The Charles Engelhard Court** to admire the windows by Tiffany, glass-maker close to the Art Nouveau movement.

Painting and sculpture – Painting during the **Colonial period** largely featured portraits and heroic scenes. From the **Hudson School**, three works stand out: the *View from Mount Holyoke, Northampton, Massachusetts, after a Thunderstorm* (1835) by Thomas Cole; *Fur Traders Descending the Missouri* (1845) by George C. Bingham; and *View of Rocky Mountains* (1863) by Albert Bierstadt. The works of the **Post-Impressionists** James McNeill Whistler (1834-1903), John Singer-Sargent (1856-1925) and Mary Cassatt (1844-1926) are at the forefront. **Sculpture** is represented by, among others, *The Mountain Man* by Frederic Remington.

78

Egyptian antiquities★★

First floor *(ground floor), rooms 100-138.* This collection, considered one of the richest in the world outside of Egypt, covers all aspects of Egyptian civilization. The objects are presented chronologically, from the predynastic period (starting from 5000 BCE) until the end of the Egyptian dynasties and the era of classical antiquity (700 AD). Among the treasures on display, note the **chapel of the Tomb of Perneb★** (2450 BCE), the Chair of Reniseneb★★ (1450 BC), a rare series of **statues of the queen Hatshepsut** (around 1500-1450 BCE) and ceremonial coffins including the **Sarcophagus of Harkhebit★**. The **Temple of Dendur★** (around 15 BCE), dedicated to the goddess Isis, was saved during the laying of the Aswan Dam and given to the US in 1965. Finally, don't miss the famous **portraits of Fayum★★** from the Roman era.

Ancient Near Eastern Art

Second floor *(first floor), rooms 400-406).* This section covers a vast geographical zone, from Turkey to Afghanistan, taking in the Caucasus Mountains to the north of the Arabian Peninsula. The antiquities date from 8000BCE to 651 AD. The diversity of cultures that emerged in this space created great artistic richness. The **Sackler Gallery** recreates an audience hall in the palace of Ashurnasirpal II at Nimrud.

Islamic art★★

Second floor *(first floor), rooms 450-464.* It starts at the beginning of the founding of Islam in the 7C, and continues to the 19C. Beautiful calligraphies sit side-by-side with marvelous miniatures, ceramics, mosaics, jewelry, and sumptuous textiles and rugs.

19C century painting and sculpture★★★

Second floor *(first floor), rooms 800-830*. No museum in the world has such a high concentration of major artists and world-famous works. **Impressionism** is one of the best represented currents here with Renoir, Monet, Manet, Corot and Degas. Among their works, don't miss Renoir's *Bouquet of Chrysanthemums* (1881) and *In the Meadow* (1888-1892). From Monet, you'll find *Poppy Fields near Argenteuil* (1875), *Haystacks* (1891), *Rouen Cathedral: The Portal* (1894), *Water Lilies* (1891). From Manet, *Boating* (1874) and *The Monet Family in Their Garden at Argenteuil* (1874). The works of **Degas**, spread over several rooms, depict his favorite subjects: female bathers and dancers and horses.

Among the **Post-Impressionists**, be sure to see, from Van Gogh, *Cypresses* (1890) and *La Berceuse* (1888-1889); from Seurat, the subtle *Parade* (*Circus Sideshow*, 1888); from Cézanne, *Bathers* (1874-1875), *The Card Players* (1890), and from Courbet, *Woman with a Parrot* (1866).

European painting★★★

Second floor *(first floor), rooms 600-644*. All the European schools of painting, from the Middle Ages to the 18C, are admirably represented.

Among the masterpieces of the **Italian schools** (Florence, Venice, Sienna), look for *The Epiphany* (1320) by Giotto, *Portrait of a Woman with a Man at a Casement* (1440) by Filippo Lippi and The Last Communion of Saint Jerome (1490) by Botticelli. You should also see *The Musicians* (1595) by Caravaggio and the canvasses by Raphael, Titian and Tiepolo. The **Spanish school** is represented by striking paintings, such as the *The View of Toledo* (1595) by El Greco, or the portrait of *Manuel Osorio Manrique de Zuñiga* (1790) by Goya. Of the **northern schools** of Flanders, Holland and Germany, be sure to see the portraits by Hans Memling, *The Last Judgement* (1425); *The Harvesters* (1565) by Bruegel; *Young Man and Woman in an Inn* (1623) by Frans Hals; *Aristotle with a Bust of Homer* (1653) by Rembrandt and the marvelous *Young Woman with a Water Pitcher* (1662) by Vermeer. The **French school** brings together *The Fortune Teller* (1630) by Georges de La Tour, *The Abduction of the Sabine Women* (1633-1634) by Poussin and Mezzetin (1718-1720) by Watteau.

Asian art★★★

Second and third floors *(1st and 2nd floors), rooms 200-253*. **Chinese art** – As well as a reconstruction of a Ming dynasty-era court, the museum presents a fine variety of Chinese funerary art, ceramics, bronze objects and **paintings**★★, covering a vast period from the neolithic era (3rd millennium BCE) to the present day. A part of the exhibit is dedicated to Tibet, with superb painted panels and a Buddha dating from the 11C.

Korean art – The lesser known Korean work features impressive vases and **ceramic and bronze utensils★★**, as well as prehistoric pottery, and particularly beautiful lacquered and encrusted cases★.

Japanese art – You will see a series of **screens★**, painted panels, **prints★★** from the 18C and 19C, elegant cases and a collection of *netsukes★*, charms which served as counterweights used for attaching small hip flasks and other items to belts.

Southeast Asia – From Nepal to India, taking in Thailand, Cambodia and Indonesia, these rooms present the pantheon of Hindu divinities and impressive Khmer sculptures.

NEUE GALERIE★

E3 1048 5th Ave. (at 86th St.) - ℘ 212 628 6200 - www.neuegalerie.org - Thur-Mon 11am-6pm (first Fri every month 8pm) - guided tour (1hr) Fri-Mon at 3.30pm - $25 (seniors $16 and students $12); free first Fri every month 5-8pm - under 12s not admitted, 12-16 year olds accompanied by an adult. Allow 1hr.

This Beaux-Arts mansion, once the home of the Vanderbilts, has since 2001 housed the Austrian and German art collections of cosmetics heir and businessman **Ronald Lauder** and of the art dealer **Serge Sabarsky**. The collection spans works by Egon Schiele, Gustav Klimt (including the precious *Portrait of Adele Bloch-Bauer I*, 1907), Oskar Kokoschka,

Kandinsky, Paul Klee and George Grosz. Look for furnishings and pieces of decorative art from the Wiener Werkstätte school.

SOLOMON R. GUGGENHEIM MUSEUM★★

E3 1071 5th Ave. - ℘ 212 423 3500 - www.guggenheim.org - Fri-Wed 10am-5.30pm (Tue and Sat 8pm) - $25 (students and seniors $18); pay what you wish Sat. 5-8pm - guided tour at 2pm.

The Guggenheim Foundation, created in 1937 by **Solomon R. Guggenheim**, is a conservatory of contemporary art and an icon of modern architecture. The edifice (1956) conceived by **Frank Lloyd Wright**, likened by some to a washing machine, takes the form of a splayed out spiral. On entering, the visitor is immediately struck by the famous helical ramp (400m/1312ft) and the glass roof. The **Kandinsky Gallery★★★** exhibits a selection of the some 200 works by the artist in the museum's permanent collection, one of the largest in the world. The **Thannhauser Collection** features 75 Impressionist and Post-Impressionist works. Among the collection, you'll find *Woman Ironing* by Picasso and *In the Vanilla Grove, Man and Horse* by Gauguin. The rest of the museum presents a rolling collection of 20C artists, including Brancusi, Calder, Marc Chagall, Paul Klee, Robert Delaunay and Joan Miró. The museum collection is also enriched by Dada pieces and surrealist works, donated by Peggy

Spiral ramp, Solomon R. Guggenheim Museum

Guggenheim; all in all, there are 6 000 works in the collection.

COOPER-HEWITT DESIGN MUSEUM★★

E3 *2 E. 91ˢᵗ St. (at 5ᵗʰ Ave.) - ☎ 212 849 8400 - cooperhewitt.org - 10am-6pm (Tue. 8pm) - $16 (students $7, seniors $10, under 19s free; pay what you wish on Tue. 6-8pm). Allow 1-2hr.*

This imposing 63-room mansion (1902) belonged to steel millionaire **Andrew Carnegie**. The museum, originally founded in 1897 in the building of the Cooper Union, moved here in 1976. It's the only American museum exclusively dedicated to **decorative arts**, with an emphasis on **design** spanning cultures, eras and continents. After three years of construction, the museum reopened in 2015 with an expanded exhibition space and a **new**, **innovative concept**: At the entrance, an interactive pen is lent to visitors to interact across 15 screens spread around the museum, navigating through the objects of the collection, including those that are not exhibited in the galleries. Back home the visitor can retrace their steps on the museum's website. Don't forget to explore the gardens, which give an idea of how the Belle Époque New York gentry lived.

JEWISH MUSEUM★

E3 *1109 5ᵗʰ Ave. (at 92ⁿᵈ St.) - ☎ 212 423 3200 - www.thejewish museum.org - Thur-Tue 11am-5.45pm (Thur. 8pm, Fri. 4pm) - closed public holidays and major Jewish holidays - $18 (seniors $12, students $8, under 18s free); free on Sat. Allow 30-60min.*

Founded in 1904 in a beautiful French Neo-Gothic edifice owned by banker **Felix Warburg**, this museum tells the story of 4 000 years of Jewish history through some 28 000 objects, including a Torah ark dating from the 12C, exquisite bindings, ancient textiles and ritual vases.

MUSEUM OF THE CITY OF NEW YORK★★

E2 *1220 5ᵗʰ Ave. (at 103ʳᵈ St.) - ☎ 212 534 1672 - www.mcny.org - 10am-6pm - closed Jan 1, Thanksgiving and Dec 25 - $20 (seniors and students $14, under 20s free).* This Neo-Georgian mansion traces the history of the city via **reconstructions of interiors★★** (17-19C), including two rooms inspired by Rockefeller's house, a collection of functional and decorative objects, as well as scale models. Maritime history and the history of the port are evoked. A collection of teddy bears and exquisite **dolls' houses★★** will delight children and grown-ups alike.

EL MUSEO DEL BARRIO★

E2 *1230 5ᵗʰ Ave. (at 104ᵗʰ St) - ☎ 212 831 7272 - www.elmuseo.org - Wed-Sat 11am-5pm, Sun 12-5pm - suggested contribution $9 (seniors and students $5; under 12s free); Free Wed for seniors.*

Created in 1969 on the edge of Harlem's Hispanic district, **El Barrio**, this museum is dedicated to Latino-American and Caribbean cultures.

It encourages the creativity of this community by displaying the work of young artists in temporary exhibitions. Its pre-Columbian and contemporary collections are rarely presented to the public.

GRACIE MANSION★

F3 East End Ave. (at 88th St.) - *℘* 212 676 3060 - www.graciemansion.org - guided tour (45min) Mon. at 10am, 11am, 5pm - advance booking required - free. This ravishing manor (1799), the official residence of the mayor of New York, is a perfect example of the Federal style, with its covered galleries and green shutters.

ROOSEVELT ISLAND TRAMWAY★

D4 2nd Ave. (at 59th St.) - rioc.ny.gov/302/tram - runs every 15min (7-8min during rush hours), 6am-2am (Fri-Sat 3.30am) - use MTA MetroCard. Parallel to Queensboro Bridge, this cable car offers a surprising view of the city. The journey only lasts a few minutes, but the capsule rises rapidly above the water's edge, providing a fine view of Manhattan (especially at night). On the other side, Roosevelt Island is far quieter than Midtown just across the river.

MT VERNON HOTEL MUSEUM AND GARDEN

E5 421 E. 61st St. (btw 1st Ave. and York Ave.) - *℘* 212 838 6878 - mvhm.org - Tue-Sat 11am-4pm - closed Jan 1, July 4, Thanksgiving and Dec 25 - walk-in

© FrankvandenBergh//iStock

Roosevelt Island Tramway by Queensboro Bridge

83

tours available - $8 (seniors and students $7, under 12s accompanied by adults free). - Allow 1hr.
Originally built as a carriage house in 1799, this stone building was converted into a day hotel in 1826. It was a popular countryside escape for New Yorkers when the city was still concentrated below 14th Street. Today, the Colonial Dames of America own and operate the property. Tours give visitors a glimpse of life in the early 19C, right as the city was experiencing rapid growth following the opening of the Erie Canal. The 18C-inspired gardens in the back provides a lovely respite from the Manhattan bustle.

Upper West Side★★ and Morningside Heights★★

Less chic than the Upper East Side, this area nonetheless remains a bastion of the intellectual elite. With Lincoln Center and its prestigious concerts and Columbia University, this is the home of many well-off liberals and is more laid-back than its rival to the east of Central Park. Here, you'll find the upper crust of the literary and artistic worlds, having lofty conversations to a soundtrack of jazz, opera and world music. The avenues are lined with bookshops and cafés with outdoor seating.

▶**Access:** Subway: Stations between Columbus Circle and Cathedral Parkway, on lines 1, 2, 3 and A, B, C, D. Bus: M7, M10, M11, M79, M86, M96, M116.
Detachable map C2-3-4, D1-2-3.

84

▶**Tip:** Start at Columbus Circle, continue on foot to the Museum of Natural History, then take the bus up to Columbia. Book in advance if you want to go to a concert at Lincoln Center.

UPPER WEST SIDE★★

Unlike the rest of the city, the Upper West Side was built from the north, on the site of Nieuw Haarlem, founded in the 17C, at the level of today's 125th St., toward the south. It was the arrival of the raised rail track that sealed its development. The creation of Columbia University (1897) made this a magnet for the intellectual elite, writers, musicians and the Jewish bourgeoisie.

COLUMBUS CIRCLE

C4 On the southwest corner of Central Park, the crossroads of Columbus Circle, dominated by the statue of Christopher Columbus (1894), marks the start of the Upper West Side. At the entrance of the park, the **Maine Monument** (1913) pays homage to the 260 sailors of the battleship *Maine* destroyed in the port of Havana in 1898. The glass-walled bar of the Mandarin Oriental hotel offers a magnificent view over the city.

MUSEUM OF ARTS AND DESIGN★

C4 *2 Columbus Circle (facing Central Park) - ✆ 212 299 7777 - www. madmuseum.org - 10am-6pm (Thur 9pm - closed Mon. and certain public holidays - $18 (seniors $14, students*

$12, under 18s free, pay what you wish Thur. from 6pm).

The MAD presents a collection of superb objects displaying elegant design, sublime sobriety or complicated embellishments. You'll find glass, ceramics, interior decorations, works of contemporary art, but also jewelry and painting, as well as objects taking unusual forms and using unusual materials (plastics, gypsum and even ash). On the 6th floor, three artists' studios are open to the public; on the 9th is chic restaurant Robert, known for its great view over Central Park.

THE SHOPS AT COLUMBUS CIRCLE

C4 The southwest of Columbus Circle is occupied by this imposing building (2004) with a concave facade. The base houses a massive shopping center, grocery store, and a diverse range of dining options. The building then splits into two 80-story glass towers, once occupied by the Time Warner offices before they moved to Hudson Yards (*p. 48*) in 2019.

LINCOLN CENTER★

C4 *Broadway, between 62nd and 66th Sts. - ℘ 212 875 5456 - www.lincolncenter.org.*
This enormous cultural complex houses 11 of the most prestigious arts institutions in New York, including five auditoriums, a library and a school. The idea to gather all these artistic venues in one place came in 1955. The construction of Lincoln

Columbus Circle

Center necessitated the razing of 188 buildings in this formerly insalubrious area, the neighborhood in which *West Side Story* was set. John D. Rockefeller III was the president of the construction committee. The central plaza sits in front of the **Metropolitan Opera House**, which hosts productions from the Metropolitan Opera and the American Ballet Theatre. On the right, the **David Geffen Hall** houses the New York Philharmonic, formerly based in Carnegie Hall. In the **David H. Koch Theater** opposite, you'll find the New York City Ballet. On the other side of 65th Street is the famous Juilliard School.

AMERICAN FOLK ART MUSEUM★★

C4 2 Lincoln Square, (Columbus Ave btw 65th and 66th Sts.) - ℘ 212 595 9533 - www.folkartmuseum.org - Tue-Thur 11.30am-7pm, Fri 12pm-7.30pm, Sat 11.30am-7pm, Sun 12pm-6pm - closed Mon and public holidays - free.
This museum was housed in a modern building next to the MoMA for 10 years before returning to its first historic home in July 2011, where the collection is displayed in rotation. Functional objects from the colonial age and the different eras of immigration are displayed with furniture, fabrics, spectacular weathervanes, naïve paintings and works of outsider art.

DAKOTA BUILDING

D3 1 West 72nd St. Home to the likes of Lauren Bacall and Judy Garland, The Dakota apartments was also where that **John Lennon** was assassinated in front of in 1980. Previously, this beautiful Neo-Gothic building served as the backdrop for *Rosemary's Baby*, directed by Roman Polanski.

NEW YORK HISTORICAL SOCIETY★★

D3 170 Central Park West (at 77th St.) - ℘ 212 873 3400 - www.nyhistory. org - Tue-Sat 10am-6pm (Fri 8pm), Sun 11am-5pm - $22 (seniors $17, students $13, 5-13 years $6); pay what you wish on Fri from 6pm. Allow 1hr. Founded in 1804 to preserve the history of the city, this institution brings together a library and a museum conserving various *objets d'art*, a fine series of paintings from the **Hudson School** and more than 400 **John J. Audubon** watercolors. Temporary exhibitions draw from the collections, selecting pieces according to themes related to the city. The recently renovated **Henry Luce III Center** on the fourth floor is organized like a storehouse for the museum, with huge glass cabinets, filled with almost 40000 objects of all kinds: games, utensils, Tiffany lamps as well as George Washington's camp bed. It is also home to the new **Center for Women's History**. Do not miss the short film *New York Story*, shown throughout the day in the first floor theater. The immersive theatrical experience is a beautiful ode the city's history and its place in the world.

AMERICAN MUSEUM OF NATURAL HISTORY★★★

D3 200 Central Park West (enter at 77th or 81st St.) - ℘ 212 769 5100 - www.amnh.org - 10am-5.45pm - closed Thanksgiving and 25 Dec - suggested admission $23 (seniors and students $18, 2-12 years $13), includes admission to the Rose Center; there are additional ticket options and prices for special exhibitions, IMAX films, or the Space Show - free tours leave from lobby 15 minutes past every hour.
The immense, magnificent **Museum of Natural History**, along with its scientific library, is one of the largest in the world. Its research center

American Museum of Natural History

specializing in biology, anthropology and astrophysics also has an excellent reputation. Started in 1874, the monument with its hodgepodge of styles was only finished in the 1930s. Its most spectacular extension is the **Rose Center for Earth and Space**★★, an impressive glass cube (2000). But it was the museum's anthropologists in particular that gave the institution its standing, carrying out many expeditions and studies at the end of the 19C and start of the 20C. The **Theodore Roosevelt Memorial Hall**★★ presents a 16.8m/55ft reconstitution of a Barosaurus skeleton. The **Hall of Biodiversity** (*ground floor*) evokes contemporary biological issues. Next is the **Hall of Ocean Life**, and then a series of rooms exploring the **environment of North America** and one more specifically dedicated to the environment of New York State. In the **Northwest Coast Hall**, exploring the indigenous cultures of this region, admire the vast cedar canoe, collections of Amerindian and Inuit craft, as well as totem poles. Coming back towards the entrance hall, finish the visit with the mammals of North America.

The back of this floor, past the **Hall of Human Biology and Evolution**, is specifically dedicated to geology, with a **Hall of Meteorites** (a major piece is the 34 t fragment of meteorite found in Greenland in 1895) and a room **dedicated to minerals and precious stones** (some 4000 specimens including the *Star of India*, a 563-carat sapphire, the largest in the world). The first floor is divided into four

themes: the **peoples of Africa**, the **peoples of Asia**, the **peoples of Latin America**, and a section dedicated to **birds**. Dioramas place animals and people in the context of the given continent. More than 60000 objects reproduce the daily life of dozens of tribes. The **birds** of the Southern Seas and from across the world are stuffed to stunning effect.

The second floor brings together rooms dedicated to ethnology, in particular the **American Indians (Native Americans) of the Eastern Woodland and the Plains**, including reconstructions of their cabins. A little further along, the superb **Hall of Pacific Peoples**, filled with beautiful pieces (and dedicated to Margaret Mead) is at once bright and intimate, making it a good place to stop for contemplation. In the animal world, you'll find reptiles, primates and birds from North America.

The third floor houses six superb **Fossil Halls**. Here you may discover the first vertebra of the dinosaurs (including a *Tyrannosaurus rex*), as well as mammals and their ancestors (mammoths, giant ground sloths).

Rose Center for Earth and Space★★ – *Space Show from 10.30am-4.30pm every 30min.* The scientific representation of the cosmos employs cutting edge audiovisual techniques. The **Space Theater** (in the Hayden Planetarium) is worth visiting just for its **Star Show**, a 3D presentation of a journey through space, refined with the help of NASA. At the foot of the sphere, **Scales of the Universe** is a 120m/394ft-long exhibition illustrating the history of our universe. A short presentation succinctly explains the Big Bang. The **Hall of Planet Earth** presents more specifically the history of our planet and its geological and climactic evolution. Finally, the **Hall of the Universe** retransmits images from the Hubble Telescope.

CATHEDRAL OF SAINT JOHN THE DIVINE★★

D2 *1047 Amsterdam Ave. (at 112ⁿᵈ St.) ✆ 212 316 7540 - stjohndivine.org - Mon-Sat 9am-5pm, Sun 12.30-2.30pm; for worship only 7.30am-6pm every day - sightseeing admission $10 (seniors and students $8). - guided tours available at additional cost.* Constructed for the Episcopal Church (1892), it can welcome up to 3 000 worshippers. Today it's also a cultural space, and hosts music and art shows. The west facade, flanked by two unfinished towers, is centered around the **Great Bronze Doors**; made by the Parisian founder who worked on the Statue of Liberty. The immense nave is punctuated with 14 bays. Behind the choir, the radiating chapels are dedicated to seven different immigrant populations in the United States. The central chapel contains a silver triptych by pop artist Keith Haring (1989). Explore the sprawling Pulpit Lawn where the three **resident peacocks** roam freely.

COLUMBIA UNIVERSITY★★

D1 *From 114ᵗʰ to 120ᵗʰ St. - main entrance on Broadway at 116ᵗʰ St. - www.columbia.edu - Visitor Center (✆ 212 854 4900) at 213 Low Library: Mon-Fri 9am-5pm - download map for self-guided visit. Visitors can walk freely around campus and in the Low Memorial Library (access to other buildings permitted only with guide).* Founded in 1754 by the English under the name King's College, it was renamed Columbia College after the American Revolution. It is a private university, and one of the most prestigious in the country and a member of the Ivy League, a group of eight very selective universities on the East Coast. It is known for its scientific departments (anthropology, genetics, biotechnology), law and business. Since 1902, it has housed a school of journalism founded by publisher Joseph Pulitzer. It is this institution that awards each year the prestigious prize of the same name. Among its famous students (and faculty) are more than 80 Nobel laureates, presidents Roosevelt and Eisenhower, Madeleine Albright, Boutros Boutros-Ghali, economists such as Alan Greenspan and Milton Friedman, and writers such as Jack Kerouac, Allen Ginsberg, Federico García Lorca, J.D. Salinger, Isaac Asimov and Paul Auster. The main buildings are spread around a vast plaza. To the north, **Low Memorial Library★** (1895) is reminiscent of Rome's Pantheon. Its interior staircase is dominated by a statue of the goddess Minerva.

*In 2016, the **Roy and Diana Vagelos Education Center**, dedicated to medicine, was inaugurated. Conceived by architectural agency Diller Scofidio + Renfro (responsible for the famous High Line), the 14-story building comprises a structure mixing steel and concrete, inside which the study rooms combine with a vertical circulation, named a "study cascade". 104 Haven Ave., corner of W. 171st St.*

Inside, you can admire the rotunda and the Beaux-Arts style décor. The brick **Earl Hall** (1902), topped with a cupola, is distinguishable by its pediment and Neoclassical columns. It houses social services and the center of religious confessions on campus. **St Paul's Chapel** is a church built in brick in Italian Renaissance style. In the basement, **Postcrypt Coffeehouse** rings with memories of the 1960s and the poems of Jack Kerouac and Bob Dylan songs. On the south side of the chapel, **Buell Hall** (1878) is all that remains of the psychiatric asylum that occupied this site before the university. Maison Française, the French cultural center of the university, is installed on the floor above. Behind, a bronze reproduction of Rodin's *Le Penseur* marks the entrance to the philosophy and French building. The **Butler Library** (1934) houses the campus library, one of the largest in the country: Here are more than 2 million of the university's 9.2-million volume collection.

RIVERSIDE DRIVE AND PARK★★

D1-2/C2-3 The park spreads out on the riverside (as the name suggests), along **Riverside Drive**, from 72nd to 155th Sts. The stretch south of 100th St is the most pleasant; do stop at the **garden and crabapple grove** (91st St.).

RIVERSIDE CHURCH★★

D1 *Riverside Dr. and 120th St. - www.trcnyc.org - 9am-5pm.* This imposing Neo-Gothic church, with its 120m/394ft bell tower, was partially financed by John D. Rockefeller. Its east portal is inspired by Chartres Cathedral in France. Inside you'll find two stained glass panels from the 16C, from the cathedral in Bruges and a chiming clock made up of 74 bells.

GENERAL GRANT NATIONAL MEMORIAL★

D1 *Riverside Dr. and 122nd St.) - 𝄞 212 666 1640 - www.nps.gov/ gegr - welcome center: daily except Mon-Tue 9am-5pm; mausoleum: daily except Mon-Tue 10am-5pm - closed Thanksgiving and Dec 25 - free.* This monument (1896) is dedicated to **Ulysses S. Grant**, president of the United States from 1869 to 1877. A vast dome covers the crypt in which niches house busts of Grant's comrades in arms. Photographs arranged across two small rooms tell the story of his life.

Harlem★

Harlem is a neighborhood of juxtapositions, with its handsome brownstones, cocktail bars, and upscale restaurants alongside crumbling public housing projects (council housing) and pockets of poverty. With Columbia University directly south and Upper West Side real estate prices driving people north, plus enticing museums and parks, Harlem gentrified rapidly and became a very desirable place to live.

▶**Access:** Subway: 125th and 135th Sts on lines A, B, C, D, 2 and 3. Bus: M1, M7, M10, M11.
Detachable map F1, E1-2.
▶**Tip:** Unless you are going to a gospel service on Sunday (come early, as space is limited), weekdays are more lively. Plan an evening in a jazz club. If you're out quite late, it's easiest to take a cab home. ♿*Our top picks/Nightlife in Harlem, p. 126.*

After the 1658 foundation of the first Dutch village (south of present-day Harlem), the surrounding area remained rural until the arrival of the railway in 1837 and then the overground subway line. Harlem is a historically black neighborhood, although real estate developers initially tried to bring in white tenants. In the 1920s, there were 60 000 black residents in Harlem, which led to some white flight and the beginnings of the area as a hub of black American culture. The birth of **jazz culture** and Prohibition made the lively clubs of Harlem the rendezvous spots of intellectuals, artists and party-makers. The fashionable bars vibrated with the sounds of jazz and blues. This was the golden age of Harlem, with the emergence of a distinct African-American identity. The end of Prohibition and the **Great Depression** (late 1929-1939) would

sound the death knell for this period. The jazz scene would move down to Greenwich Village, while the middle classes were beset by unemployment and left the area, leaving it to be occupied by a more disadvantaged population. The ensuing degradation and extreme poverty in the area meant it subsequently acquired a bleak reputation as a dangerous place. During the 1960s, the raising of black political consciousness would cast Harlem in the spotlight once more, due in part to the passionate political speeches delivered by **Malcolm X** in the Black Muslim Temple of Islam (he was assassinated in 1965 on 166th St.). Harlem gave New York its first black mayor, David Dinkins. Slowly at first and then more quickly, the area was built up: new shops started opening, new apartment towers went up, and the historic brownstones were renovated and restored. The neighborhood has retained a strong black identity, but with rents and housing prices increasing, many lower income residents continue to move to less costly neighborhoods in other boroughs.

STUDIO MUSEUM IN HARLEM★

E1 144 W. 125*th* St. - ☏ 212 864 4500 - www.studiomuseum.org - main location closed for construction till 2021, temporary space 429 W. 127*th* St. - Thur-Sun 12-6pm.
Since 1968, this museum, dedicated to Afro-American and other local artists, has held fine temporary exhibitions, 92 ranging from folk art to video and more conceptual installations.

MARCUS GARVEY PARK★

F1-2 Heading south, between West 124th and 119th Sts, you'll walk the length of this steep and pretty park. On the west side, you'll see a row of well renovated brownstones, allowing you to imagine the bourgeois Harlem of the end of the 19C.

APOLLO THEATER★

E1 253 West 125*th* St. - www.apollotheater.org.
In 1914, this historical icon of jazz did not permit black people to enter. In 1934, it took its present-day name, becoming a temple of black music and welcoming Louis Armstrong, Aretha Franklin, Ray Charles, James Brown and even The Jackson 5.
Amateur Night (Wednesdays) has

been the starting place of huge talents. Renovated in 2002, the Apollo has once more become one of the hottest venues in town.

SCHOMBURG CENTER FOR RESEARCH IN BLACK CULTURE★

F1 515 Malcolm X Blvd. (near W. 135*th* St.) - ☏ 212 491 2200 - www.nypl.org/locations/schomburg - Mon-Sat 10am-6pm.
The Puerto Rican **Arthur Schomburg** (1874-1938) amassed a collection of documents and artifacts that told the story of Afro-American history, heritage and identity. The center functions as a leading research library — with more than 5 million documents on black culture — and hosts regular public programs including literary festivals, photography exhibitions, jazz concerts and more.

STRIVERS ROW

F1 West 138*th* and 139*th* Sts.
These beautiful brownstones are where the rising black bourgeoisie of the 1920s lived in Georgian and Neo-Renaissance style residences.

MORRIS-JUMEL MANSION

Off map (by E1) 65 Jumel Terrace (btw 160*th* and 161*st* Sts.) - ☏ 212 923 8008 - www.morrisjumel.org - Tue-Fri 10am-4pm (Sat-Sun 5pm) - closed Mon and public holidays - $10 (seniors and students $8, under 12s free).

© Rolf Schulten/imageBROKER/age fotostock

Apollo Theater

This manor house (1765) is the last testament of the Pre-Revolutionary Period. During the War of Independence (1776), it would house the headquarters of **George Washington**. The Federal style house was bought by the **Jumels**, rich French traders.

HISPANIC SOCIETY OF AMERICA★

Off map (by E1) *613 W. 155ᵗʰ St. - ✆ 212 926 2234 - www.hispanic society.org - currently closed for renovation.*
This little museum offers a fascinating look at Hispanic civilization going back to the Pre-Roman era and houses a rich collection of master works. The gallery on the ground floor contains an impressive selection of traditional and ritual objects, pieces of silverware, prehistoric tools, Renaissance recumbent statues and spun fabrics. To the right, don't miss the room dedicated to **Joaquín Sorolla y Bastida** (1863-1923): here you'll find 14 monumental paintings executed between 1911 and 1919 illustrating Spanish traditions and customs.

The **upper gallery** exhibits a fine collection of ceramics, pottery and jewelry and is decorated with a number of **portraits** by Le Greco, Morales, Ribera, Vélasquez and Goya.

The Cloisters★★★

Perched on a hill dominating the banks of the Hudson, north of Washington Heights, this museum reproduces the architecture of a fortified European monastery. Inside, the medieval art collection is set amid cloisters dismantled on the Old Continent and reconstructed here in New York. The serene complex displays the art of the Middle Ages to admirable effect.

▶**Access:** Subway: 190th St (followed by 10 min. walk or bus M4)
Fort Tryon Park – ✆ 212 923 3700 - www.metmuseum.org/visit/met-cloisters - Mar-Oct 10am-5.15pm (Nov-Feb 4.45pm) - closed 1 Jan, Thanksgiving and 25 Dec - $25 combination ticket with Met (♿ p. 74) and Met Breuer (♿ p. 72). *Detachable map. off map around E1*.
▶**Tip:** A great spot for a picnic. Allow 1-1hr30min for the visit.

THE CLOISTERS★★

During his travels, sculptor **George Barnard** collected architectural vestiges of the south of France. In 1925, **John D. Rockefeller** donated sufficient money to the Metropolitan Museum to acquire this collection, to which he would add more works. He then constructed a museum of the Middle Ages in Tryon Park (1938).
Roman art is showcased in the Romanesque Hall and in *The Fuentidueña Apse* (Castille, 1160). The *Saint-Guilhem Cloister* (Hérault, end of the 12C) is an example from the very origins of Gothic architecture.
Gothic art can be appreciated in its full splendor with *Langon Chapel* (Moutiers-Saint-Jean Abbey, 13C), the *Abbey of Saint-Michel-de-Cuxa* and the *Chapter House from Notre-Dame-de-Pontaut*. On the lower level, a Gothic chapel houses the tombs of Catalogne et d'Aragon (13-14C). The *Bonnefont Cloister* (France, 13-14C) sits next to a medieval garden opening onto the Hudson. The *Cloister from Trie-en-Bigorre* (end of 15C) evokes the contemplative atmosphere of a monastery.

THE COLLECTIONS★★★

The **Glass Gallery** brings together a series of stained glass windows, statues and a Flemish altarpiece depicting the Nativity (Rogier Van der Weyden, 15C). The **treasury** brings together a collection of sacred objects: *cloisonné* enamel from Limoges (13C), Rosary beads (Holland, 16C), embroidered tapestries, illuminated manuscripts of *Riches Heures du duc de Berry*, golden pedestal salt cellars and rock crystal (Paris, 13C). The collection of **tapestries** contains some of the oldest in the world (15-16C), including *The Hunt of the Unicorn*, from the Château de Verteuil-sur-Charente. Further rooms house stained glass, altarpieces and Gothic statues, as well as the Annunciation Triptych, by Flemish master Robert Campin (15C).

Brooklyn★★ and Queens★

Brooklyn is much larger than Manhattan, so much so that if not part of NYC, it would be the US's fourth-largest city. It's a curious mix of ultra hip, chic and working-class. Each neighborhood offers something a little different: Dumbo is lofts, luxury towers, and Manhattan skyline views, Williamsburg is the seat of bobos, Park Slope is familial, Red Hook quiet and full of warehouses but rapidly becoming popular. North of Brooklyn, Queens is the true American melting pot; more than half of Queens residents speak a language other than English. This is where cinema was born, where new museums are opening and where artists are moving in.

▶**Access:** Almost all subway lines go to Brooklyn and Queens. The numbers of the bus lines that serve Brooklyn are preceded by B, Q for Queens. To get around Queens, take buses or subway lines E, G, N, R and 7. Brooklyn and Queens both have ferry ports (www.ferry.nyc) - one-way $2.75, free transfers available).

Area map p. 96. Detachable map BC8, F4, E5-7-8, G5.

▶**Tip:** If you have time, get up early, or stay up late, and cross the Brooklyn Bridge on foot.

BROOKLYN★★

Brooklyn's history goes almost as far back as that of Manhattan. This once rural area was made part of New York in 1898. Today it is the most populated of New York's boroughs (almost 2.6 million inhabitants), with a mix of people and styles. It's a **multicultural** place, shaped by the historical installation of immigrant communities, and also houses a number of trendy, upscale areas, such as **Brooklyn Heights**.

On sunny days, the lawns of **Prospect Park** and the beaches of **Coney Island**, to the south, are packed with New Yorkers seeking a little vitamin D.

BROOKLYN HEIGHTS★★

At the time of the American Revolution, this part of Brooklyn served as the headquarters for **George Washington**. Subsequently it became the first area to be developed when transfers to Manhattan became easier. The **promenade**, which overlooks the river, offers a beautiful **view★★★** over Lower Manhattan and its skyscrapers.

WILLIAMSBURG★

E7-8 Williamsburg is the hip shop window of Brooklyn, originally the haven of artists driven out of Manhattan by skyrocketing prices. The reputation of the area and its laid-back cool vibe, which has now been well and truly cultivated, has made it so desirable that prices have gone through the roof, and the idea of it being an artistic sanctuary is no more than an illusion.
Head there on the weekend, when flea markets enliven the area, attracting a steady stream of young tattooed types in flannel shirts, would-be models and entertained onlookers. Turn onto Bedford Ave. and Berry St., north of the **Williamsburg Bridge**. From the bridge (walk or cycle across) linking the Lower East Side to Brooklyn and the banks of the East River, you can enjoy a fine view of Midtown Manhattan.

DUMBO★
BROOKLN BRIDGE PARK★★

Situated between Brooklyn and Manhattan Bridges, **Dumbo** *(Down Under the Manhattan Bridge Overpass)* is a former warehouse and factory district that changed rapidly in the early 2000s, taken over by young professionals and families. From **Brooklyn Bridge Park★★** situated on the riverside (once called Empire Fulton Ferry Park), you can admire the unforgettable vista of the towers of Manhattan.

PROSPECT PARK★

Three entrances: 150 Eastern Parkway, 455 Flatbush Ave., 990 Washington Ave. - www.prospectpark.org.
This green space, designed by the architects and landscapers of Central Park, features stretches of grass and groves, with a more bucolic, rustic feel than its big brother. During summer, many concerts are performed here.

Brooklyn Botanic Garden★ - *990 Washington Ave. - www.bbg.org - Mar-Oct, Tue-Fri 8am-6pm, Sat-Sun 10am-6pm; Nov, Tue-Fri 8am-4.30pm, Sat-Sun 10am-4.30pm; Dec-Feb, 10am-4.30pm - $15 (free Fri. before noon in Mar-Nov and weekdays in Dec-Feb); $25 combined ticket with the Brooklyn Museum.* Open year round, the garden spans 52 acres and is especially popular in the spring when the cherry blossoms bloom in the Japanese garden.

BROOKLYN MUSEUM OF ART★★

200 Eastern Parkway - ✆ 718 638 5000 - www.brooklynmuseum.org - Wed-Sun 11am-6pm (Thur 10pm, first Sat. each month 11pm) - closed Jan 1, Thanksgiving and Dec 25 - suggested admission $16 (seniors and students $10, under 19s free); $25 combined ticket with Botanic Garden (seniors and students $16); additional prices for special exhibitions.
The Brooklyn Museum (1897) has one of the richest collections in the city. Its works, spread over 52 000 m²/559 723 ft², (the museum's

Brooklyn by Union Street

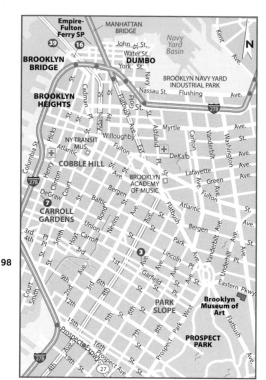

BROOKLYN

```
0        3/10 mi
0            600m
```

WHERE TO EAT

Al di La .... ③
Grimaldi's .... ⑯
River Café .... ㊲

WHERE TO DRINK

Brooklyn Farmacy
& Soda Fountain .... ⑦

Also see Williamsburg
on the detachable map.

whole collection comprises 1.5 million pieces) are of the highest caliber. Their temporary exhibitions are some of the best in town. Unless you want to limit your visit to one particular theme, start on the 5th floor.

American painting and sculpture★★★ – *5th flr.* The key themes in this series of works are the geography, ethnicities and everyday life of the country. Expect landscape

paintings, genre paintings, depictions of the War of Secession, exoticism, self-taught painters, artists from the great art schools, the passage from the romantic 19C to the industrial 20C, abstract expressionism, and the minimalism of the later half of the 20C.

Decorative arts★★ – *4th flr.* Here you'll find reconstitutions of interiors in different styles across different eras, the oldest being a Dutch interior from the 17C. You will also see the eclecticism that marked transition from the 19C to the 20C, from the Neo-Gothic to Japanese influence, followed by Arts & Craft, Art Nouveau, and Art Deco.

Elizabeth A. Sackler Center for Feminist Art★ – *4th floor.* This original department focuses on art seen and made by women on their own terms. The central work is **The Dinner Party**★★ (1974-1979), an impressive installation by Judy Chicago.

Egyptian antiquities★★★ – *3rd flr.* These collections, among the most reputable in the world, bring together fascinating everyday objects. The first part presents the history, with the second explaining the different facets of daily life in Egypt during Antiquity.

European painting★★ – *3rd flr.* This part of the exhibit, laid out around the arcaded cloister, is a walk through 700 years of European painting, including landscapes, portraits and historical or genre scenes, from artists such as Monet, Courbet and Sorolla.

Art from Asia and the Islamic World ★ – *2nd flr.* The arts of various Asian civilizations are on display here (China, Korea, Japan, India, Nepal, and Southeast Asia) and Arabic (Islamic Art). The *1st floor* is dedicated to temporary exhibitions and houses pricey restaurant The Norm.

NEW YORK TRANSIT MUSEUM

99 Schermerhorn St. (Enter through a subway entrance at street level) - ℘ 718 694 1600 - www.nytransitmuseum.org - Tue-Fri *10am-4pm, Sat-Sun 11am-5pm - closed on public holidays - $10 (Over 62s and 2-17 years $5) - Under 15s must be accompanied by an adult.*
Located in a decommissioned subway station in downtown Brooklyn, this museum takes visitors through the history of New York's storied transit system. Explore vintage buses and subway cars; complete with retro advertisements.

QUEENS★

The most spread out of the five boroughs of New York, Queens, along with Brooklyn, occupies the west part of Long Island. This is where we find two of New York's three airports: JFK and LaGuardia. This is also the home of two of the city's sporting temples, Citi Field and Flushing Meadows, which hosts the US Tennis Open. In the 1920s, the Astoria district was home to around 20 film studios. Today, after having long been disdained, multicultural Queens is turning the explosion of prices in Manhattan to its advantage, attracting artists, young creators, businesses and visitors, the latter who come for its fascinating museums.

MOMA PS1★

E5 *22-25 Jackson Ave. - moma.org/ps1 - Thur-Mon 12pm-6pm - closed 1 Jan, Thanksgiving and 25 Dec - suggested admission $10 (seniors and students $5, unders 17s free) - Food on site.*
This artistic center, dedicated to contemporary art, is part of MoMA,

working in conjunction as an incubator for young artists. Housed in a former school constructed in Neo-Renaissance style at the start of the 1890s, it has retained its sombre shell. The contrast is striking between the austerity of the brick walls, endless corridors, and preserved school furniture and the audacity of the exhibitions presented between the walls of the old classrooms. You'll find paintings featuring distorted bodies, audacious installations and unsettling abstract conceptual videos: it is hard to find a common thread, but impossible not to have some kind of reaction to this fairly exhaustive spread of contemporary art today. The future stars of the MoMA may well be among the exhibited artists.

MUSEUM OF THE MOVING IMAGE★★

G5 36-01 35*th* Ave. (corner of 36*th* St.), Astoria - ☏ 718 777 6888 - www.movingimage.us - Wed-Sun 10.30am-5pm (Fri 8pm, Sat-Sun 6pm), - $15 (seniors and students $11, 3-17 years $9); free Fri. from 4pm.
This museum, featuring costumes and photographs of legendary actors, is located in the former film industry district, on the site of Astoria Studios. Various photos tell the story of the golden age of the studios, but it is above all the permanent exhibit *Behind the Screen* that will enthral children, teens and adults alike. In the immaculately white rooms, you'll find close to 130 000 nostalgia-inducing objects (cameras, décor, costumes, wigs, etc.), from the Chewbacca costume in *Star Wars* to the scary mannequin of *The Exorcist*. Early arcade games are exhibited (including the legendary *Tron*) and a cinema revisiting Ancient Egypt is recreated. Interaction is built in to the exhibits, with the opportunity to try your hand at the techniques of dubbing, making your own animated film, or even creating the soundtrack of a Hollywood blockbuster. A fascinating and educational visit, great fun for kids and adults.

NOGUCHI MUSEUM★

F4 9-01 33*rd* Rd., Long Island City - ☏ 718 204 7088 - www.noguchi.org - Wed-Fri 10am-5pm, Sat-Sun 11am-6pm - closed Jan 1, Thanksgiving and Dec 25. - $10 (seniors and students $5, Under 12s free); free 1st Fri of every month.
Isamu Noguchi (1904-1988), a great American sculptor of Japanese origin, Noguchi is famous for his gardens (UNESCO, Paris), his public spaces (Hart Plaza, Detroit), his playgrounds (Playscape, Atlanta), his objects (the famous paper and bamboo Akari lamps) and his theater sets (Balanchine, Martha Graham). The museum presents samples of his sculptures, as well as the sculptures of other contemporary artists. It also organizes a roster of photography and design exhibitions.

Addresses

Smith & Mills
© Paul Wagtouicz/Smith & Mills

🍴

Where to eat

At any hour of the day, you can find something inexpensive to eat, even in the most upscale districts (for a picnic, almost any supermarket is a good bet). You will never be short on restaurant choices. On the weekends, do as New Yorkers do and indulge in brunch. ♿ *Where to drink p. 112 and Eating out p. 138.*

♿ Find the addresses on our maps using the numbers in the listing (ex. ❶). The coordinates in red (ex. C2) refer to the detachable map (inside the cover).

104 LOWER MANHATTAN

Area map p. 16-17

Around $ 20
❶❸ **Adrienne's Pizzabar – *A8*** - 54 Stone St. - Ⓜ *Wall St.* - ☎ 212 248 3838 - www.adriennespizzabarnyc. com - 11.30am-11pm (Thur-Sat 12am, Sun 10pm) - mains $17/$22. Delicious pizzas as well as oven dishes and salads.

From $20 to $40
❶⓪ **Pier A Harbor House – *A8*** - 22 Battery Pl. - Ⓜ *Bowling Green* - ☎ 212 785 0153 - www.piera.com - ♿ - Sun-Wed 11am-12am, Thur-Sat 11am-2am - mains $16/$36. At the tip of Manhattan, this historic establishment-turned-restaurant features a large terrace with uninterrupted views of the boats and the Statue of Liberty. Great seafood,

including an excellent *mi-cuit* tuna burger and tasty fish & chips.

CHINATOWN

Area map p. 31

Less than $ 20
❶ **Nom Wah Tea Parlor – *B7*** - 13 Doyers St. - Ⓜ *Canal St.* - ☎ 212 962 6047 - nomwah.com/chinatown - 10.30am-10pm (Thur-Sat 11pm) - mains $6/$14. The city's oldest dim sum parlor since 1920 stays fresh with timeless dishes and vintage decor.

From $30 to $50
㉕ **Peking Duck House – *B7*** - 28 Mott St., #A - btw Chatham Sq. and Pell St. - Ⓜ *Canal St.* - ☎ 212 227 1810 - www.pekingduckhousenyc.com - ♿ - 11.30am-10.30pm (Fri-Sat 11.45am-11pm) - mains $35/$44. The crispy-skinned Peking duck ($54) wrapped in pancakes is a treat not to be missed.

NOLITA

Area map p. 36

Less than $20
⓱ **Lovely Day – *B7*** - 196 Elizabeth St. - Ⓜ *Bowery* - ☎ 212 925 3310 - www. lovelydaynyc.com - 11am-11pm (Fri-Sat 12am) - mains $8/$17. Floral wallpaper, red moleskin banquettes and stools and a vintage tile floor look more diner than Thai, but the Thai food here is superb.

From $20 to $30

21 Mottsu – *B7* - 285 Mott St. (btw Houston and Prince Sts) - Ⓜ Prince St. - ✆ 212 343 8017 - www. mottsu. com - 11.30am-11pm (Fri 11.30pm, Sat 12-11.30pm, Sun 12-11pm) - mains $11/$26. Excellent Japanese food. Expect maki, sushi and other fish-based dishes.

41 Seamore's – *B7* - 390 Broome St. - Ⓜ Spring St. - ✆ 212 730 6005 - www.seamores.com - ♿ - 12-10pm - mains $16/$29. Beachy vibes and the freshest seafood; all sourced sustainably. You can't go wrong with the Montauk scallops pasta or the Baja fish tacos. The cocktails are excellent, too.

TRIBECA AND SOHO

Area map p. 31

Around $20

1 Bubby's – *A7* - 120 Hudson St. - Ⓜ Franklin St. - ✆ 212 219 0666 - www.bubbys.com - 8am-11pm (Fri-Sat 12am) - mains $18/$24. A great family brunch spot serving all the best American comfort foods: pancakes, pies, biscuits and, of course, burgers.

1 Jack's Wife Freda – *B7* - 224 Lafayette St - Ⓜ Spring St. - ✆ 212 510 8550 - jackswifefreda.com - 8.30am-11pm (Fri-Sat 12am, Sun 10pm) - mains $12/$28. American-Mediterranean dishes and classic cocktails in an understated all-day bistro. The green shakshuka or Freda's matzo ball soup will not disappoint.

From $30 to $50

48 Troquet – *B7* - 155 Grand St. - Ⓜ Canal St. - ✆ 212 343 4295 - troquetnyc.com - 11.30am-1am (Sat-Sun 10.30am-1am) - mains $19/$32. Behind Troquet is the story of two friends with a New York City dream; they brought on chef Camille Martin, who previously worked at a Pourcel brothers' restaurant in Sri Lanka. In this cute, hip Parisian-style bistro, you'll find well-executed Franco-American cuisine accompanied by a fine wine menu and rounded off with a warm, inviting atmosphere.

LOWER EAST SIDE

Area map p. 36

From $20 to $40

29 Russ & Daughters – *C7* - 179 East Houston St. - Ⓜ 2nd Ave. - ✆ 212 475 4880 - www.russanddaughters.com - 8am-6pm (Thur. 7pm) - mains $12/$24. Loyal customers come here for the chewy bagels, extra-creamy cream cheese and smoked fish.

11 Freemans – *B7* - Freeman Alley - Ⓜ Bowery - ✆ 212 420 0012 - www.freemansrestaurant.com - ♿ - 11am-11pm (Sat-Sun 2am) - mains $18/$33. This restaurant, decorated in the style of a country hunting lodge, serves great rustic dishes.

1 Ivan Ramen – *C7* - 25 Clinton St. - Ⓜ Delancey/Essex St. - ✆ 646 678 3859 - www.ivanramen.com - 12.30-10pm (Fri-Sat 11pm) - mains $16/$20. Chef Ivan Orkin serves up excellent ramen, original izakaya dishes and international craft beers in a fun, casual setting. On nice days, opt for a table in the back patio.

🍴
GREENWICH VILLAGE

Area map p. 41

Up to $20

① by CHLOE. – *B6* - 185 Bleecker St. - Ⓜ *West 4 St.* - ☏ *212 254 3000* - *eatbychloe.com* - Mon- Fri 11am-11pm; Sat-Sun 10am-11pm - mains $5/$10. A fashionably casual vegan chain. Great salads, a solid veggie burger, and lots of other yummy plant-based options.

From $20 to $40

😋 ㉞ Mary's Fish Camp – *B6* - 64 Charles St. - Ⓜ *Christopher St.* - ☏ *646 486 2185* - *www.marysfish camp.com* - 12pm-3pm, 6pm-11pm, Sun 12pm-4pm - mains $15/$32. Noisy but convivial atmosphere in this restaurant that celebrates seafood from the East Coast, including grilled sea bass, mussels, clams and lobster rolls.

⑮ Roey's – *B6* - 1 Perry St. - Ⓜ *14th St.* - ☏ *646 864 1200* - *roeysnyc.com* - Mon-Fri. 12-10pm, weekends 10am-10pm - mains $14/$18. The menu at this modern Italian meets California restaurant entices with pizza (broccoli rabe with stracciatella, pine nuts, pecorino); assorted hearty salads, and simple vegetables like roasted carrots with pumpkin seeds, maple ricotta. It's *very* popular and recommended for brunch. Good for families (kids' menu, books, toys).

From $50 to $100

① Carbone – *B7* - 181 Thompson St. - Ⓜ *Houston St.* - ☏ *212 254 3000* - *carbonenewyork.com* - 11.30am-2pm, 5.30-11.30pm - mains $34/$57.

Completely over the top in the best way possible. Come for a show (the delightful choreography between the entire waitstaff and you, the unsuspecting audience, can't be called anything but), stay for the delicious Italian-American dishes the servers in burgundy tuxes keep putting in front of you.

① Minetta Tavern – *B6*- 113 Macdougal St. - Ⓜ *West 4 St.* - ☏ *212 475 3850*- *www.minettata vernny.com* - lunch Wed-Fri 12-3pm; dinner daily 5pm-12am (Thur-Sat 1am); brunch Sat-Sun 11am-3pm - mains $24/$65. Classic New York lives on in this bustling tavern. The Black Label burger is worth every dollar. As does the roasted bone marrow.

EAST VILLAGE

Less than $20

① Le Fournil – *C6* - 115 2nd Ave. - Ⓜ *Astor Pl.* - Tue-Sat 11.30am-7.30pm - $3/$8. This French bakery has big shoes to fill after taking over the space of the beloved Moishe's. With his buttery croissants, hefty rye loaves and savory sandwiches, the new owner and third-gen baker from Normandy will be just fine.

⑳ Momofuku Noodle Bar – *C6* - 171 1st Ave. - Ⓜ *Astor Pl.* - ☏ *212 777 7773* - *momofukunoodlebar.com* - lunch 12-4.30pm (Sat-Sun 4pm); dinner 5.30-11pm (Fri-Sat 12am); - mains $13/$17. Seating along a counter. The menu includes smoked chicken wings, Chinese buns and assorted noodles.

From $20 to $30

27 Supper – *C7* - *156 East 2nd St. - M 2nd Ave. - ℘ 212 477 7600 - www. supperrestaurant.com - ⌦ - Mon-Thur 4pm-12am, Fri 4pm-1am, Sat 10am-1am, Sun 10am-12am - mains $18/$25.* Décor is understated and warm. Excellent North Italian food. A fine terrace for sunny days.

CHELSEA

Up to $20

7 Chelsea Market – *B6* - *75 9th Ave - at 15th and 16th Sts. - M 8th Ave. - ℘ 212 652 2111 - www.chelseamarket.com - Mon-Sat 7am-2am, Sun 8am-10pm.* Here you'll find all the ingredients for an excellent picnic: fresh or dried fruit, pastries, sandwiches, soups, salads and more. If the weather isn't so great, you can sit here or choose one of the little restaurants. Very busy on weekends.

24 Café Serai – *B6* - *150 W. 17th St. - in the Rubin Museum of Art - M 18th St. - ℘ 212 620 5000 - www. rubinmuseum.org - Thur-Mon 11am-5pm (Fri. 10pm) - closed Jan 1, Thanksgiving and 25 Dec - mains $10/$19.* Excellent wraps, salads and dishes with a North Indian and Tibetan influence. Don't miss the hearty *momos* (dumplings).

From $20 to $30

6 Cookshop – *B5* - *156 10th Ave. - at 20th St. - M 23rd St. (8th Ave.) - ℘ 212 924 4440 - www.cookshopny. com - Mon-Fri 8am-11pm, Sat 10am-11pm, Sun 10am-10pm - closed 25 Dec - mains $23/$28.* Cuisine made from ingredients brought from producers in the Hudson Valley and in Vermont. The menus and décor offer elegant simplicity.

UNION SQUARE AND MADISON SQUARE

Up to $20

2 Eisenberg's – *C6* - *174 5th Ave. - 22nd and 23rd St. - M 23rd St. - ℘ 212 675 5096 - www.eisenbergsnyc.com - 6.30am-8pm, Sat 9am-6pm, Sun 9am-5pm - under $20.* This deli, opened in 1929, has defied fashions and fads, consistently offering generous helpings of substantial, well-executed fare. The setting is unchanging, but the sandwiches are always excellent (especially the pastrami and tuna). An excellent option in this area where it's hard to find good food at modest prices.

35 Shake Shack – *C6* - *Southeast corner of Madison Square Park (at. E. 23rd St. and Madison Ave.) - M 23rd St (Broadway). - ℘ 212 889 6600 - www. shakeshack.com - 9am-10pm - under $20.* This location is where Danny Meyer's high-end fast food chain all started. If you're craving a hot dog or burger, you won't be disappointed (quality brioche buns, well-seasoned meat). Pair with a frozen custard shake or draft beer.

From $20 to $30

8 Eataly – *C6* - *200 5th Ave. - M 23rd St. (Broadway)- ℘ 212 229 2560 - www.eataly.com - ♿ - 9am-11pm.* A vast temple dedicated to Italian gastronomy: produce, meats, seafood, bread and pastries and several restaurants. Rooftop bar.

🍴

47 **abcV** – *C6* - *38 E. 19th St. -* Ⓜ *23rd St. - ☎ 212 475 5829 - www.abchome.com/dine/abcv - Mon-Fri 8-10.30am, 12-3pm; Sat-Sun 11am-3pm; dinner 5.30-10.30pm (Thur-Sat 11pm, Sun 10pm) - plates $9/$18.* Jean-Georges Vongerichten's third restaurant inside the ABC home store. Food so flavorful, the fact that its all vegetarian is a happy afterthought. Cool interior.

MIDTOWN WEST

Up to $20

😊 **36** **Kung Fu Kitchen** – *C4* - *811 8th Ave. (at 49th St.)-* Ⓜ *42nd St. - ☎ 917 388 2555 - www.kfdelicacy.com - 10.30am-10.30pm - under $20.* Welcome to the kingdom of noodles! Peter Song, the chef who you'll see rolling out noodle dough behind a glass pane, is a specialist. The noodles are eaten in soups or stir fries. Excellent dumplings.

1 **The Deco** – *C5* - *231 W. 39th St. -* Ⓜ *Times Sq.-42 St. - ☎ 646 993 1650 - thedeconewyork.com - Mon-Fri 7am-9pm, Sat-Sun 8am-9pm.* A brand new food hall filled with local vendors from all five boroughs and a bar spotlighting New York brews. All within glitzy 1920s interiors.

From $30 to $50

22 **Nobu 57** – *CD4* - *40 W. 57th St. -* Ⓜ *57th St. - ☎ 212 757 3000 - www.noburestaurants.com - 11.45am-2.15pm, 5.45-11.15pm - mains $33/$42.* In a softly-lit, sleek setting, enjoy high-end Japanese cuisine, including the famous miso cod.

MIDTOWN EAST

From $20 to $30

1 **Her Name is Han** – *C5* - *17 E. 31st St. -* Ⓜ *33 St. - ☎ 212 779 9990 - www.hernameishan.com - 12-2.30pm, 5.30-10.15pm (Thur-Sat 11.15pm, Sun 9.15pm) - mains $23/$29.* Korean comfort food with a modern twist in a homey spot. Also great Korean spirits.

From $30 to $50

😊 **23** **Oyster Bar** – *C5* - *89 E. 42nd St. - in Grand Central Terminal -* Ⓜ *Grand Central - ☎ 212 490 6650 - www.oysterbarny.com - ♿ - Mon-Sat 11.30am-9.30pm - mains $29/$38.* An unbeatable Midtown spot for fresh seafood. Fantastic happy hour deals,

CENTRAL PARK

From $20 to $40

3 **The Loeb Boathouse** – *D3* - *E. 72nd St. -* Ⓜ *72nd St. - ☎ 212 517 2233 - www.thecentralparkboathouse.com - Mon-Fri 12pm-3.45pm, 5.30-9pm; Sat-Sun 9.30am-3.45pm, 6-9pm - mains $18/$26.* In the heart of Central Park, this romantic restaurant and its veranda offers the best views of the sun setting on the water — and the food is great.

UPPER EAST SIDE

From $20 to $30

18 **Maya** – *E4* - *1191 1st Ave. -* Ⓜ *Lexington Ave. - ☎ 212 585 1818 - www.eatmaya.com - Mon-Fri 4-11pm, Sat 10am-11pm, Sun 10am-10pm -*

© Max Lau/The Deco

109

The Deco

mains $16/$30. Mexican cuisine, harmoniously blending tradition and contemporary, is a served in a refined but welcoming setting.

UPPER WEST SIDE

Up to $20

37 **Whole Foods Market** – *C4* - *10 Columbus Circle - in the basement level of the shopping center -* Ⓜ *59th St. -* ☎ *212 823 9600 - 7am-11pm.* Quality produce, fruit and veg, cheeses, breads, etc. Eat on the premises or take it to nearby Central Park. You'll find themed hot and cold food bars (Indian, Mexican, Japanese) where you can fill up your own containers, buffet-style.

From $20 to $30

1 **Barney Greengrass** – *D3* - *541 Amsterdam Ave. -* Ⓜ *86 St. -* ☎ *212 724 4707 - www.barneygreengrass. com -* 🍴 *- Tue-Sun 8.30am-4pm (Sat-Sun 5pm) - mains $13/25.* This Jewish deli has been serving the best sturgeon since 1908. Packed with locals on weekend mornings, it's always a great scene.

From $60 to $240

4 **Jean-Georges** – *C4* - *1 Central Park West (in Trump Tower) -* Ⓜ *59thSt./Columbus Circle -* ☎ *212 299 3900 - jean-georgesrestaurant.com -* ♿ *- 11.45am-2.30pm, 5-11pm - set menus $68 (lunch)/ $238.* American cuisine from Michelin triple-starred Jean-Georges Vongerichten, in

🍴

an exceptionally elegant space. Extremely professional service. The lunch menu offers very good value: Four dishes for around $60.

BROOKLYN - WILLIAMSBURG

Area map p. 98

Up to $20

39 **Grimaldi's** – *B8* - *1 Front St. -* Ⓜ *York St. -* 🖋 *718 85 84 300 -* *www.grimaldis-pizza.com -* ⊠ ♿ - *11.30am-8.30pm - dishes less than $20.* Under the Brooklyn Bridge, this restaurant is famous for its pizzas. It's very popular with hungry bridge-walkers, so expect a long line.

1 **Pierozek** – *D3* - *592 Manhattan Ave. -* Ⓜ *Nassau Ave. -* 🖋 *718 576 3866 - pierozekbrooklyn.com - Tue-Thur 11am-8pm, Fri-Sun 11am-9pm - dishes $5/$12.* Venture to Greenpoint for classic pierogis. Recipes and come straight from its older sister restaurant in Poland. Complete with the traditional sides: red borscht, croquette and beer.

From $20 to $40

1 **Juliette** – *E7* - *135 N. 5th St. -* Ⓜ *Bedford Ave. -* 🖋 *718 388-9222 - juliettewilliamsburg.com - 10.30am-11pm (Fri-Sat 12am) - mains $16/27.* French bistro meets Williamsburg vibes with plants overflowing in the main dining room and the roof deck perfect for warmer days. Yes, the food's good too.

😊 **42** **Fette Sau** – *E7* - *354 Metropolitan Ave. -* Ⓜ *Metropolitan Ave. -* 🖋 *718 963 3404 - www. fettesaubbq.com - 12-11pm (Mon*

5-11pm) - dishes $22/$38. Expect excellent American barbecue with pork ribs, grilled beef and sausages from heritage breeds raised naturally on small farms. For sides, try the broccoli salad. The vibe is relaxed, featuring big tables, around which diners eat with their hands, in a hangar that opens onto the road.

😊 **49** **The Four Horsemen** – *E7* - *295 Grand St. -* Ⓜ *Metropolitan Ave. -* 🖋 *718 599 4900 - fourhorsemenbk. com - 5.30pm-12am - dishes $13/$32.* The restaurant from the singer James Murphy (of LCD Soundsystem) opened in June 2015, and has been a resounding success. The concept is inventive small plates to share, comprising surf and turf, and an impressive selection of natural wines.

46 **Al Di La** – *248 5th Ave. -* Ⓜ *Union St. -* 🖋 *718 783 4565 - www.aldilatrattoria.com - Mon-Fri 12pm-3pm, Sat-Sun 11am-3pm; dinner Mon-Sat 5.30-10pm (Fri-Sat 11pm), Sun 5-10pm - mains $19/$29.* This *trattoria* is a firm favorite with locals . From the antipasto to the desserts, everything is pitched just right, with distinct and powerful flavors. You'll find authentic Italian-style pasta, with the choice of more ambitious dishes such as braised rabbit. Great décor with a charming touch of old-fashioned charm.

More than $60

28 **River Café** – *B8* - *1 Water St. -* Ⓜ *York St. -* 🖋 *718 522 5200 - www. rivercafe.com -* 🅿 *on reservation - 5.30-11pm, Mon-Fri 8.30am-11.30am, Sat-Sun 11.30am-2.30pm - fixed menu $72 lunch / $150 dinner.* Breathtaking

Barney Greengrass

view of Manhattan and excellent cuisine. After 4pm, suit jackets obligatory for men and ties preferred.

26 Peter Luger – **D8** - *178 Broadway (at Driggs Ave.)* - Ⓜ *Marcy Ave.* - ✆ *718 387 7400 - www. peterluger.com -🚭 🅿 ♿ - Mon-Sat 11.45am-9.45pm (Fri-Sat 10.45pm, Sun 12.45pm-9.45pm - dishes $51/$97.* A carnivore's dream. Reservation essential. Wear loose trousers.

QUEENS

Up to $20

1 Court Square Diner – **E5** - *45-30 23rd St.* - Ⓜ *Court Square-23 St.* - ✆ *718 392 1222 - courtsquarediner. com - Open 24 hours - dishes $8/$20.*

It's all retro vibes in this family-run diner that has been a mainstay in Long Island City since 1946. A block from MoMA PS1 (♿*p.99*), the staff happily serve classic American diner fare to regulars and tourists alike.

From $20 to $40

38 Ornella – **H3** - *29-17 23th Ave.* - Ⓜ *Astoria Blvd* - ✆ *718 777 9477 - www. ornellatrattoria.com - 12pm-10pm, Thur-Sat 12pm-11pm - mains $20/$25.* A *trattoria* known for the excellent quality of its products (stuffed clams, meatballs, pasta).

Where to drink / Take a break

New York offers a plethora of cafés, wine bars, bakeries and rooftops where you can take a break and have a drink. Note that all bars are 21+, but restaurants with bars allow guests of all ages.

♦ Find the addresses on our maps using the numbers in the listing (ex. ❶). The coordinates in red (ex. C2) refer to the detachable map (inside the cover).

LOWER MANHATTAN

Area map p. 16-17
😊 ⓰ **The Dead Rabbit** – *A8* - *30 Water St.* - Ⓜ *Whitehall St./South Ferry* - 📞 *646 422 7906* - *www.deadrabbitnyc.com* - *11am-4am, Sat-Sun 10am-3am* - *cocktails $16.* "World's Best Bar" three years running. Behind an anonymous looking facade hides the den of two Northern Irish friends, who are revolutionizing the cocktail bar scene. On the ground floor is an authentic Irish tavern (with a suitably long list of whiskeys). Upstairs, mixologists take wicked delight in turning patrons' taste buds upside down.

NOLITA

Area map p. 36
❶ **Morgenstern's Finest Ice Cream** – *B7* - *2 Rivington St.* - Ⓜ *Bowery* - 📞 *212 209 7684* - *www.morgensterns nyc.com* - *12pm-11pm (Fri-Sat 12am).* The creamiest ice cream in inventive flavors like Vietnamese coffee and burnt sage.
❸ **Café Habana** – *B7* - *17 Prince St. (at Elizabeth St.)* - Ⓜ *2nd Ave.* - 📞 *212 625 2001* - *www.cafehabana. com* - *9am-12am (Mon-Wed 11pm, Sun 10pm).* Expect *muy caliente* atmosphere in this Cuban spot where visitors savor cocktails and empanadas.
㉛ **Eileen's Special Cheesecake** – *B7* - *17 Cleveland Pl. (at Kenmare St.)* - Ⓜ *Spring St.* - 📞 *212 966 5585* - *www.eileenscheesecake.com* - *Mon-Fri 9am-9pm, Sat-Sun 11am-8pm.* The richest, creamiest cheesecakes in dozens of flavors.

TRIBECA - SOHO

Area map p. 31
😊 ㉟ **Grand Banks** – *A7* - *Pier 25 - Hudson River Park* - Ⓜ *Franklin St.* - 📞 *212 660 6312* - *www.grandbanks.org* - *Open Apr-Oct* - *Mon-Tue 11am-12.30am, Sat-Sun 10am-12.30am.* This schooner dating from 1942 is today the city's most popular boat-bar-restaurant serving seafood. The

oysters are excellent, but getting a table is near-miraculous, though you can always come for a drink and admire the magnificent view over New Jersey and the skyscrapers of the Financial District. Magic at sunset. The wait can be long.

5 **Smith & Mills** – *A7* - *71 N. Moore St. (at Greenwich St.) -* Ⓜ *Franklin St. -* ☎ *212 226 2515 - www.smithandmills. com - Sun-Wed 11am-2am, Thur-Sat 11am-3am.* With its retro accents and tasty cocktails, this tiny bar is a must.

21 **Houston Hall** – *B6* - *222 W. Houston St. -* Ⓜ *Houston St. -* ☎ *212 675 9323 - www.houstonhallny.com - Mon-Tue 4pm-1am, Wed-Thur 12pm-2am, Fri-Sat. 12pm-3am, Sun 12pm-8pm.* This American-scale establishment with exposed brick and beams gives you a lot of bar for your buck. With its huge cask, this bar feels welcoming despite its size (as long as you don't mind crowds and sports screens).

25 **Macao** – *B7* - *311 Church St. -* Ⓜ *Canal St. -* ☎ *212 431 8642 - www.macaonyc.com - 5pm-2am (Thur-Sat 4am).* This former opium den is something of a New York sensation; the sign and outside appearance contrast with the opulence of the interiors, set across two floors. Décor is a revisit to traditional Chinese aesthetic and the cocktails are creative.

27 **Pegu Club** – *B7* - *77 W. Houston St. -* Ⓜ *Bleecker St. -* ☎ *212 473 7348 - www.peguclub.com - 5pm-2am (Fri-Sat 4am).* Expect intimate ambiance in this long, narrow bar where you'll sip on excellent cocktails (the Champagne concoctions are

particularly good). Look out for the discreet entrance: Only a little sign announces the place — go through the door and upstairs. Live music on some evenings.

32 **Azul On The Rooftop** – *A7* - *Hotel Hugo (*🍸 *p. 128) - 525 Greenwich St. -* Ⓜ *Spring St. -* ☎ *212 608 4848 - www.azulrooftop.com - Mon-Thur 5pm-11pm, Thur-Sat 5pm-12.30am.* Not the most spectacular of the rooftops, but it is one of the most secret. Expect soft armchairs, wood paneling and a fun atmosphere with a Cuban twist. Uninterrupted views over the Hudson and Soho.

LOWER EAST SIDE

Area map p. 36

113

6 **Dudley's** – *C7* - *85 Orchard St. -* Ⓜ *Delancey St. -* ☎ *212 925 7355 - www.dudleysnyc.com - 9am-12am (Fri-Sat 2am, Sun-Mon 11pm).* Corner bar with long bay windows onto the street, pretty bohemian décor and jazzy soundtracks. Cocktails, beers and (biodynamic) wines, and food served at all hours. Simple and effective.

7 **Il Laboratorio del Gelato** – *C7* - *188 Ludlow St. -* Ⓜ *2nd Ave. -* ☎ *212 343 9922- www.laboratorio delgelato.com - 7.30am-10pm (Fri 12am), Sat 10am-12am, Sun 10am-10pm.* A little shop with the creamy gelato plays directly on to the "laboratory", where some 75 flavors, spanning the classic to the more experimental, are made.

☺ **28** **Mr Purple** – *C7* - *180 Orchard St., -* Ⓜ *2ⁿᵈ Ave. -* ✆ *212 237 1790 - www.mrpurplenyc.com - 4pm-2am (Thur-Fri 4am), Sat 11am-4am, Sun 11am-2am).* Located on the 15ᵗʰ floor of Hotel Indigo, this bar offers a 360° view over the city. Patrons can choose to stay sheltered behind the glass bay window and enjoy the sparkle of the Manhattan skyscrapers, or head on to the terrace, in front of the (largely decorative) heated pool, sipping on beautifully crafted cocktails.

GREENWICH VILLAGE

Area map p. 41

8 **Magnolia Bakery** – *B6* - *401 Bleecker St. (at W. 11ᵗʰ St.) -* Ⓜ *Christopher St. -* ✆ *212 462 2572 - www.magnoliabakery.com - 9am-10.30pm (Fri-Sat 11.30pm).* Immortalized by *Sex and the City*, this bakery sells cupcakes, cheesecakes and more delicious desserts.

1 **Marie's Crisis Cafe** – *B6* - *59 Grove St. -* Ⓜ *Christopher St. -* ✆ *212 243 9323 - mariescrisis.us -*🖥 *6pm-11.30pm, Fri 5pm-12am, Sat 6pm-12am.* Dive bar meets piano bar in this storied place. Especially popular for the show tunes.

1 **Boba Guys** – *B6* - *11 Waverly Pl. -* Ⓜ *Astor Pl. -* ✆ *415 967 2622 - www.bobaguys.com - 12-9pm (Fri-Sat 10pm).* Exceptionally high standards for milk, loose-leaf tea, and tapioca pearls makes this San Francisco bubble tea chain especially popular amongst NYU students in the neighborhood. Consider a non-traditional option like their horchata.

EAST VILLAGE

Area map p. 36

10 **Mudspot** – *C6* - *307 E. 9ᵗʰ St. -* Ⓜ *Astor Pl. -* ✆ *212 228 9074 - www.mudnyc.com - 7.30am-12am, Sat-Sun 8am-12am.* Great little all-hours café, which is a good spot for brunch, a snack or an evening drink.

22 **Ten Degrees** – *C7* - *121 St. Marks Pl. -* ✆ *212 358 8600 - www.10degrees bar.com - 4pm-4am, Fri 1pm-4am, Sat-Sun 12pm-4am.* Hip wine (and cocktail). The décor is very of-the-moment with wood cabinets, brick walls and salvaged pieces. From 12-8pm, drinks are two for the price of one. Charcuterie and cheese boards available.

12 **Anyway Café** – *C7* - *34 E. 2ⁿᵈ St. (at 2ⁿᵈ Ave.) -* Ⓜ *2ⁿᵈ Ave. -* ✆ *212 533 3412 - www.anywaycafe.com - 12pm-2am (Fri-Sat 4am).* On a quiet side street, patrons here sip on vodka while nibbling on blinis.

CHELSEA/MEATPACKING

Area map p. 41

☺ **36** **The Top of The Standard** – *B6* - *848 Washington St. -* ✆ *212 645 7600 -* Ⓜ *8ᵗʰ Ave. - www.standard hotels.com/new-york -* ♿ *- 4pm-12am.* The panoramic bar of The Standard hotel is one of the most popular in New York. Chic interiors with stripped-back design. You must have a drink on the terrace at sunset, taking in the magnificent view. In the evening, access is often restricted to celebrities and VIPs; very crowded on weekends.

UNION SQUARE AND MADISON SQUARE

㉖ 230 Fifth – *C5* - *230 5th Ave. (at W. 27th St.) -* Ⓜ *28 St. -* ℘ *212 725 4300 - www.230-fifth.com -* ♿ *- 2pm-2am, Sat-Sun 10am-12am.* A rooftop bar recommended for its impressive view of Empire State Building and the skyscrapers of Midtown. Great for weekday happy hour on a warm, sunny evening.

❶ Breads Bakery – *C6* - *18 E. 16th St.-* Ⓜ *Union Square -* ℘ *212 633 2253 - www.breadsbakery.com - 6.30am-9pm (Sat 8pm), Sun 7.30am-6pm.* One of the best-reputed bakeries in the city — try the chocolate babka. Coffee and sandwiches also available.

⓮ Max Brenner – *C6* - *841 Broadway -* Ⓜ *Union Square -* ℘ *646 467 8803 - www.maxbrenner.com - 9am-12am (Fri-Sat 2am, Mon-Tue 1am).* Pots filled with steaming concoctions and a menu of almost exclusively chocolate-based treats.

㉓ Lillies – *C6* - *13 E. 17th St. -* ℘ *212 337 1970 - www.lilliesnyc.com -* ♿ *- 12pm-4am (Sat-Sun 11am-4am.* Expect old-fashioned windows, wood paneling, antiques, a monumental fireplace, ornate hanging lanterns and a marble counter. It's Victorian elegance with an undeniably contemporary indie rock soundtrack.

㉙ Old Town Bar – *C6* - *45 E. 18th St. -* Ⓜ *Union Square -* ℘ *212 529 6732 - www.oldtownbar.com - 11.30am-1am (Mon 12am), Sat 12pm-1am, Sun 11.30am-1am - closed 25 Dec.* This old-school bar, one of the oldest in the city, has been entertaining its clients since 1882. In the image of the most beautiful English pubs, it has real soul with its wood paneling, mirrors and old-fashioned light fixtures.

MIDTOWN WEST

⓯ Sarabeth's – *D4* - *40 Central Park S. -* Ⓜ *5th Ave. -* ℘ *212 826 5959 - www.sarabethsrestaurants.com -* 🅿 ♿ *- 8am-11pm (Sun 10pm) - closed 25 Dec.* Ideal for a breakfast or cake stop near Central Park. The pastries are exquisite.

㉞ Bar 54 – *C5* - *Hotel Hyatt Centric Times Square New York, 135 W. 45th St.-* Ⓜ *47-50 Sts.-Rockefeller Center Station -* ℘ *646 364 1234 - 4pm-1am (Thur-Sat 2am).* Funky music and a 1970s atmosphere reign in the city's highest rooftop bar. Magical views of the colorful illuminated skyscrapers of the city (special mention to the Chrysler Building). Impressively, the heaving city down below seems silent from here.

UPPER EAST SIDE

⓱ Dylan's Candy Bar – *D4* - *1011 3rd Ave. (at 60th St.) -* Ⓜ *59th St. -* ℘ *646 735 0078 - www.dylans candybar.com - 10am-9pm (Fri-Sat 11pm) - closed Thanksgiving and 25 Dec.* In this spot serving milkshakes, candy, and all things sugary, it's hard to resist the treats on offer, whatever your age.

⓲ Serendipity 3 – *D4* - *225 E. 60th St. -* Ⓜ *59th St. -* ℘ *212 838 3531 - www.serendipity3.com - 11.30am-12am (Fri-Sat 1am).* Kitsch décor in this café-tea room, which is also a restaurant. Kids love it.

🏺

⑲ Café Sabarsky – *E3* - *Neue Galerie, 1048 5th Ave. -* Ⓜ *86th St. -* ☎ *212 288 0665 - www.neuegalerie.org - 9am-9pm (Mon and Wed 6pm).* The museum's elegant Viennese café serves delicious pastries in a refined atmosphere befitting the handsome space.

UPPER WEST SIDE

⑳ Hungarian Pastry Shop – *D2* - *1030 Amsterdam Ave. (at 111th St.) -* Ⓜ *Cathedral Parkway -* ☎ *212 866 4230 - 7.30am-10.45pm, Sat-Sun 8.30am-10.30pm.* Opposite the Cathedral of Saint John the Divine (☞p.89), this friendly Hungarian café has been used by a number of filmmakers and has a loyal neighborhood following.

BROOKLYN - WILLIAMSBURG

Area map p. 98

① Loosie Rouge– *D8* - *91 S. 6th St. -* Ⓜ *Marcy Ave. -* ☎ *718 309 0231 - www.loosierouge.com - 6pm-2am, Sat-Sun 11am-2am.* Midcentury modern furnishings with Parisian and New Orleans touches. Live music (most nights) and cocktails on tap make it easy for a laidback evening.

😊 ㉝ Westlight – *E7* - The William Vale, *111 N. 12th St. -* Ⓜ *Nassau Ave. -* ☎ *718 307 7100 - westlightnyc. com - 12pm-12am, Sat 2pm-2am, Sun 2pm-12am.* Westlight (on the 22nd floor) does things big. Expect pretty people, stunning views over Brooklyn and the skyscrapers of Manhattan, a chic yet cozy ambiance and pared-down design. The cocktails are excellent.

😊 ㉚ Radegast Hall & Biergarten – *D7* - *113 N. 3rd St. -* Ⓜ *Bedford Ave. -* ☎ *718 963 3973 - www.radegast hall.com - 12pm-2am (Mon 4am), Sat-Sun 11am-4am.* A real *biergarten*, without the Bavarian folklore. There are two spaces; a dimly-lit wood-lined bar (around which jazz concerts are organized) and a vast room with a retractable roof and long wooden tables. Wide range of beers and food like pretzels and sausages, as well as more surprising options such as *moules-frites*.

㉗ Brooklyn Farmacy & Soda Fountain – *Off map* - *513 Henry St. (at Sackett St.) -* Ⓜ *Bergen St. -* ☎ *718 522 6260 - www.brooklyn farmacyandsodafountain.com - 11am-10pm (Fri 11pm), Sat 10am-11pm, Sun 10am-10pm.* This former pharmacy features apothecary counters where you'll find souvenirs and "made in Brooklyn" gourmet sauces. Specialties of the venue include the sundaes and the egg cream; an ice cream made from chocolate syrup, milk and seltzer. Very popular.

🛍 *Shopping*

Where to buy

For an afternoon of shopping in the department stores, head to Midtown and the Upper East Side. You'll find luxury boutiques on Madison Avenue, on 57th Street and in Soho. Fifth Avenue brings together a range of shops. For hippie and neopunk fashions, head for East Village, Lower East Side, and Williamsburg/Greenpoint. Art galleries and high-end homewares can be found in Chelsea, Soho, Nolita and Tribeca.

What to bring back

New-York themed souvenirs invade tourist shops around Times Square and 5th Avenue. Available in **department stores**, the main American brands offer items only available in the US. The best bargains in fashion and home goods can be found in **specialist outlet stores**, such as Century 21. The **thrift stores** are the best of the best in New York, and dressing in Fifties, Sixties or Eighties vintage fashions is the height of cool in trendy circles. **Sports shops** sell sneakers, American team jerseys and general streetwear.

Museum shops sell posters, models of objects, and art books. Compared to Europe, the prices of **electronics**, are favorable, particularly computers and phones. Don't forget to add the 8.875 % sales tax.

⚑ Find the addresses on our maps using the numbers in the listing (ex. ❶). The coordinates in red (ex. C2) refer to the detachable map (inside the cover).

LOWER MANHATTAN

Area map p. 16-17

❶ **Century 21** – *A8* - *21 Dey St. (btw Church St. and Broadway)* Ⓜ *Cortland St. - ✆ 212 227 9092 - www.c21stores.com - 7.45am-9pm (Thur-Fri 9.30pm), Sat 10am-9pm, Sun 11am-8pm* - Department store dedicated to discount designer clothing and accessories. You will need to rummage, but you can find great bargains.

❸⓪ **Midtown Comics** – *B8* - *64 Fulton St. -* Ⓜ *Fulton St. - ✆ 212 302 8192 - www.midtowncomics.com - 10am-8pm, Wed 8am-8pm, Sat 11am-9pm, Sun 12-7pm.* A must for fans of the Marvel universe. You'll find T-shirts and superhero merchandise, but mega-fans will head for the fanzines and first editions.

NOLITA

Area map p. 36

❷ **INA Nolita** – *B7* - *21 Prince St. (btw Elizabeth and Mott Sts.) -* Ⓜ *Spring St. - ✆ 212 334 9048 - www.inanyc.com - 12pm-8pm (Sun 7pm).* Luxury thrift store selling womenswear; garments are little-worn and in good condition; good value.

1 Roman and Williams Guild – *B7* - *53 Howard St.* - Ⓜ *Canal St.* - ℘*212 852 9099* - *rwguild.com* - *9am-11pm.* The flagship store of local interior design legends. It's no surprise the two-story space is filled with a global curation of homewares and accessories. Downstairs, there are Phaidon art books for sale. On the first storey, there's a cafe to linger a while. Before you leave, pick up a wild bouquet from the flower shop out front.

TRIBECA

Area map p. 31

3 Philip Williams Posters – *A7* - *122 Chambers St.* - Ⓜ *Chambers St.* - ℘ *212 513 0313* - *postermuseum.com* - *10am-7pm - closed Sun and 25 Dec.* Old posters of movie stars and legendary brands. Retro and OTT style.

15 Canal Street Market – *B7* - *265 Canal St.* - Ⓜ *Canal St.* - *canalstreet. market* - *10am-10pm (Sun 6pm).* An indoor market dedicated to gastronomy, art, design, fashion and beauty across multiple themed spaces.

SOHO

Area map p. 31

5 Prada – *B7* - *575 Broadway (at Prince St.)* - Ⓜ *Prince St.* - ℘ *212 334 8888* - *www.prada.com* - *11am-7pm (Sun 6pm).* The surreal architecture is the draw here, conceived by Rem Koolhaas. An airy design with a huge curve of wood resembling a skate ramp. This was once the Whitney Museum.

16 Nike – *B7* - *529 Broadway* - Ⓜ *Prince St.* - ℘ *646 716 3740* - *www.nike.com/us/en_us/retail/en/nike-soho* - *10am-8pm (Wed-Sat 9pm).* With its giant screens, works from local artists and carefully-curated design, a visit to the famous brand's store is an immersive experience. The highlight is a basketball court on the fifth and final floor, where you can take a pair of shoes for a test run.

13 Kith – *B7* - *337 Lafayette St.* - Ⓜ *Broadway-Lafayette.* - ℘ *646 648 6285* - *kith.com* - *10am-9pm (Sun 8pm).* A luxury boutique riding the wave of vintage-style sneakers being back in fashion. A number of rare models available. You'll also find quirky items.

6 Uniqlo – *B7* - *546 Broadway (near Spring St.)* - Ⓜ *Prince St.* - ℘ *877 486 4756* - *www.uniqlo.com* - *10am-9pm (Sun 8pm).* You'll find all the creativity of contemporary Japanese fashion in this low-price store. You'll also find different color variations of cashmere sweaters, impeccably-cut jackets and trousers and artist-designed graphic tees.

119

LOWER EAST SIDE

Area map p. 36

8 Economy Candy – *C7* - *108 Rivington St. (btw Ludlow and Essex Sts.)* - Ⓜ *Essex St.* - ℘ *212 254 1531* - *www.economycandy.com* - *9am-6pm, Sat-Mon 10am-6pm.* Here you'll find shelves upon shelves of candy, chocolate bars and dried fruits, with no-sugar options available.

🛍️

1 CW Pencil Enterprise – *BC7* - *15 Orchard St. -* Ⓜ *E. Broadway -* ✆ *917 734 8117 - cwpencils.com -* *11am-7pm Sat-Sun 12-7pm.* If there was such a thing as a pencil heaven, it'll look something like this. Rows and rows of neatly stacked pencils and related accesories from around the world. The sticker room in the back is a particular delight.

GREENWICH VILLAGE

Area map p. 41

10 C.O. Bigelow – *B6* - *414 6th Ave.* *(btw 8th and 9th Sts.) -* Ⓜ *W. 4th St. -* ✆ *212 533 2700 - www.bigelow* *chemists.com - 7.30am-9pm, Sat* *8.30am-7pm, Sun 8.30am-5.30pm.* This is the oldest pharmacy in the United States, dating from 1838. In completely retro environs, you'll find the best international cosmetic lines, as well as the C.O. Bigelow traditional apothecary products in their snazzy packaging: rose balm, cream with lemon extract, mint soap and essential oils.

36 Murray's – *B6* - *254 Bleecker St.* *- between 6th and 7th Ave -* Ⓜ *Christopher St. -* ✆ *212 243 3289 -* *www.murrayscheese.com - Mon-Sat* *8am-9pm, Sun 9am-6pm.* A cheese-lover's paradise. There are no less than 350 kinds of cheese from Europe and the United States. You can eat at the cheese bar here or get tasty, ample sandwiches to go.

1 Follain – *B6* - *92 Greenwich Ave.* *(at 12th St.)* Ⓜ *14th St. (7th Ave.) -* ✆ *646 896 1050 - follain.com -* *11am-7pm, Sun 12-6pm.* Clean

(non-toxic) beauty brands line minimalist shelves. The understated interior paired with friendly and helpful staff makes this place feel like a sanctuary.

EAST VILLAGE

Area map p. 36

😊 32 John Varvatos – *C7* - *315 Bowery (at Bleecker St) -* Ⓜ *Astor Pl. -* ✆ *212 358 0315 -* *www.johnvarvatos.com - 12pm-8pm,* *Sat 11am-8pm, Sun 12pm-6pm.* An (expensive) fashion boutique in what was CBGB, a legendary rock club where Blondie and the Ramones started out. Some cry sacrilege, while others make rock pilgrimages here: the designer has aimed to preserve the spirit of the site, with the original walls and stage kept intact.

1 John Derian – *C7* - *6 E. 2nd St.* *(at Bowery) -* Ⓜ *2nd Ave. -* ✆ *212 677* *3917 - www.johnderian.com -* *11am-7pm - closed Monday.* A high-end treasure trove full of weird and whimsical home goods. For a truly special NYC souvenir, pick up a handmade decoupage

CHELSEA - MEATPACKING

18 Angel Thrift Shop – *B6* - *48 W. 22nd St. -* Ⓜ *23rd St. -* ✆ *212 229* *0546 - angelstreetthrift.org -* *11am-7pm, Sat 10am-7pm, Sun* *12pm-5pm.* The proceeds of this second-hand store go to charities helping drug addicts, HIV-positive people and those with mental health

120

problems. Brands and individuals donate clothing, furniture and accessories. Some beautiful pieces at unbeatable prices.

㉞ Anthropologie – *B6* - *Chelsea Market, 75 9th Ave.* - Ⓜ *14th St.* - ✆ *212 620 3116* - *www.anthropologie. com* - *10am-9pm (Sun 8pm)*
Inside Chelsea Market is an outpost of this bobo chain, and it makes shrewd use of the industrial architecture of the site. You'll find exclusive bohemian-style clothing, accessories and homewares in a simple, timeless style. Also sells beauty products and shoes.

UNION SQUARE

⑲ Strand – *C6* - *828 Broadway (at 12th St.)*- Ⓜ *14th St.-Union Sq.* - ✆ *212 473 1452* - *www.strandbooks. com* - *9.30am-10.30pm.* A bookshop set across three levels offering cut prices; you'll find well-thumbed art books, foreign literature and all other kinds of assorted books, as well as a rare books section on the third floor. A great spot to get NYC gifts.

MIDTOWN WEST

㉑ Macy's – *C5* - *151 W. 34th St.* - Ⓜ *34th St.-Herald Sq.* - ✆ *212 695 4400* - *https://l.macys.com/new-york-ny* - *10am-10pm (Sun 9pm).*
Practically anything you might want to buy can be found at Macy's, from big designer brands to dog collars. Between floors 8 and 9 is an original wooden escalator. ⓒ *p. 54.*

㉒ B & H – *B5* - *420 9th Ave. (near 34th St.)* - Ⓜ *34th St.-Penn Sta.* - ✆ *212 615 8820* - *www.bandh.com* - *9am-7pm (Fri 1pm), Sun 10am-5pm - closed Sat and certain public holidays.*
An address for image professionals. A vast choice of photo and video materials. Smart prices on refurbished goods.

MIDTOWN EAST

㉔ Saks Fifth Avenue – *C5* - *611 5th Ave. (btw 49th and 50th Sts.)* Ⓜ *5th Ave./53rd St.* - ✆ *212 753 4000* - *www.saksfifthavenue.com* - *10am-8.30pm, Sun 11am-7pm - closed on Easter, Thanksgiving and Dec 25.* A legendary name, opened in 1924. Here

© littleny/iStock

Macy's

🛍

you'll find all the upscale designers and big brands, set over ten floors.

25 Brooks Brothers – C5 - *346 Madison Ave. (at 44th St.) - Ⓜ 42nd St.-Grand Central Term.- ☏ 212 682 8800 - www. brooksbrothers.com - 8am-8pm, Sat 9am-7pm, Sun 11am-7pm - closed Thanksgiving & 25 Dec.* This chic tailor dressed the actors of the 1950s and dresses businesswomen and men today. You'll find made-to-measure or partially made-to-measure suits, ties and more.

23 NBA Store – C5 - *545 5th Ave. - Ⓜ 42nd St.-Grand Central Term. - ☏ 212 457 3120 - nba.com/nycstore - 10am-8pm (Sat 9pm).* Accessories, team kits, and gear for basketball fans.

UPPER EAST SIDE

29 Bloomingdale's – D4 - *1000 3rd Ave. and 59th St. (you can enter on Lexington Ave.) - Ⓜ 59th St.-Lexington Ave - ☏ 212 7052 000 - www. bloomingdales.com - 10am-8.30pm, (Thur 9.30pm), Sun 11am-7pm. - closed Easter Sunday.* One of the most popular department stores because you can find just about everything there. Take a shopping break with fro-yo on the seventh floor.

1 Creel and Gow – D4 - *131 E. 70th St. - Ⓜ 68th St. - ☏ 212 227 9092 - creelandgow.com - 10am-6pm - closed Sunday.* A tiny boutique on ground floor of a classic townhouse is filled with an eclectic mix of rare specimens, curious and antiques collected from around the globe.

BROOKLYN - WILLIAMSBURG

1 Catbird – E7 - *219 Bedford Ave. - Ⓜ Bedford Ave. - ☏ 718 599 3457 - www.catbirdnyc.com - 12-8pm (Sun 6pm), Sat 11am-7pm.* Williamsburg's favorite indie jewelry spot. Look for delicate rings, bracelets and necklaces handmade by local designers.

1 Spoonbill & Sugartown Books – E7 - *218 Bedford Ave. - Ⓜ Bedford Ave. - ☏ 718 387 7322 - www. spoonbillbooks.com - 10am-10pm.* Indie bookstore with a focus on used, rare, and out-of-print art and design titles. It's cozy and easy to lose track of time in here.

37 Beacon's Closet – F8 - *23 Bogart St. - Greenpoint - Ⓜ Nassau Ave. - ☏ 718 417 5683 - beaconscloset. com - 11am-8pm - closed 1 Jan , 4 Jul, Thanksgiving and 25 Dec.* In this giant thrift store you'll unearth vintage treasures for a handful of dollars. There are other outposts around the city, but this is by far the biggest.

122

Nightlife

As a general rule, **Downtown** (to the south of 30th St.) is the most lively part of Manhattan in the evenings: there is amusement for every taste. Midtown West, with **Broadway** and **Times Square**, is the theater district. The **Upper West Side** is still the place for quality concert halls, including Lincoln Center. To the north, **Harlem** is the home of jazz and blues. **27th and 28th Streets** (between 10th and 11th Avenues) is the go-to clubs that open, change name and go out of fashion at a head-spinning speed. Be warned that the drink prices are in line with the area's reputation aka they're steep.

If you want an unforgettable experience, go to **Harlem** for a gospel mass (Sunday 9am to 11pm). They last 1hr with a mix of sermons and song (plan to bring change for the collection).

In **Brooklyn,** the bars and clubs of **Williamsburg, Greenpoint, and Bushwick** are hot and trending.

Magazines (online) New York Magazine, Time Out New York, The New Yorker, and The Village Voice (free) list concerts, shows and films.

Online box office – www.todaytix.com.

TKTS Kiosks – Times Square (W. 47th St., at Broadway and 7th Ave.). - matinee show 10am-2pm (11am-3pm Sun), evening show 3pm-8pm (7pm Sun); South St. Seaport (190 Front St., at John St.) - 11am-6pm; and Lincoln Center (61 W. 62nd St.) - 12-7pm (Sun 5pm) - arrive at least 30min before start time. Tickets sold at 25 to 50% discount for shows next day or same day. Payment by cash or card.

♿ Find the addresses on our maps using the numbers on the listings (ex. ❶). The coordinates in red (ex. C2) refer to the detachable map (inside the cover).

SOHO

Area map p. 31

❶ **SOB's (Sound of Brazil)** – **B6** - 204 Varick St. - Ⓜ Houston St. - ℘ 212 243 4940 - sobs.com - ♿ - staring from 7pm. Warm atmosphere and soft lighting. nightly concerts, salsa, samba, reggae and hip-hop. Friday, enjoy salsa classes; Saturdays are "Caribbean Saturdays" with DJs.

LOWER EAST SIDE

Area map p. 36

❷ **The Box** – **C7** - 189 Chrystie St. - Ⓜ Bowery, 2nd Ave. - ℘ 212 982 9301 - www.theboxnyc.com - from 11pm - closed Sun and Mon. This café-theater aims to recreate the atmosphere of an old-school cabaret; expect burlesque numbers, contortionists, puppets and tap dancers. Entertainment guaranteed!

❸ **Bowery Ballroom** – **B7** - 6 Delancey St. - Ⓜ Bowery - ℘ 718 514 9451 - www.boweryballroom. com A concert hall, one of the best in New York, and a bar, where famous rock groups play as well talented newcomers. Great acoustics.

GREENWICH VILLAGE

Area map p. 41

4 **55 Bar** – *B6* - *55 Christopher St. (at 7th Ave.) - Ⓜ Christopher St. - ℘ 212 929 9883 - www.55bar.com - 1pm-4am.* In a little room dating from the Prohibition period, expect nightly quality jazz and blues concerts.

5 **Village Underground** – *B6* - *130 W. 3rd St. (near 6th Ave.) - Ⓜ W. 4th St. - ℘ 212 777 7745 - thevillageunderground.com - 9am-2am - closed Tue.* This is a legendary space from the Sixties and Seventies when Bob Dylan, Joan Baez and Simon & Garfunkel played here. Intimate club known for its eclectic programming.

22 **Café Wha?** – *B6* - *115 Macdougal St. - Ⓜ W. 4th St. - ℘ 212 254 3706 - cafewha.com - 8pm-3am.* One of the most famous live music venues in the city. Opened in the 1950s, this is where luminaries such as Bob Dylan started (with his first fee said to be $16), as well as Jimi Hendrix, Janis Joplin and many others. The poets of the Beat Generation, including Ginsberg, recited poems here and some of the greatest American comedians have performed here. A performance at the legendary Café Wha? is still an obligatory rite of passage for rising stars today.

EAST VILLAGE

8 **Joe's Pub** – *C6* - *425 Lafayette St. (btw E. 4th St. and Astor Pl.) - Ⓜ Astor Pl. - ℘ 212 539 8778 - www.joespub. com - from 7pm.* An intimate venue where you can drink and eat, with rich and varied programming. Alice Coltrane, Norah Jones, Hawksley Workman and Jamie Cullum have all played here.

CHELSEA - MEATPACKING

Area map p. 41

9 **Highline Ballroom** – *B6* - *431 W. 16th St. (btw 9th and 10th Aves.) - Ⓜ 23rd St. - ℘ 212 414 5994 - highlineballroom. com - &. - 11am-11pm (Fri-Sat 4am).* A beautiful space with a dance floor and well-researched programming, from hip hop to electro: Rahzel, Ellen Allien, Mos Def, Lou Reed and Hot Chip have all passed through here.

1 **Nublu Classic** – *C7* - *62 Ave. C (at E. 5th St.) - Ⓜ Delancey/Essex St. - www.nublu.net - From 9pm.* A tiny club with its own record label. Opened by Swedish-Turkish saxophoninst Ilhan Ersahin, every night is different; from Brazilian music to experimental jazz.

UPPER WEST SIDE

11 **The West End Lounge** – *D2* - *955 West End Ave. (at 107th St.) - Ⓜ Cathedral Parkway 110th St. - ℘ 212 531 4759 - thewestendlounge.com - 8am-12am.* Excellent jazz, blues and rock club.

HARLEM

12 **Apollo Theater** – *E1* - *253 W. 125th St. - Ⓜ 125th St. - ℘ 212 531 5300 - www.apollotheater.org - opening hours vary depending on shows.* This is *the* legendary venue for jazz, R&B and soul. The famous Wednesday concerts *(Amateur Night, from 7.30pm)* are the place to catch the next big thing. 👤 *Harlem, p. 91.*

13 **Canaan Baptist Church** – *E2* - *132 W. 116th St. (near Adam Clayton Blvd.) - Ⓜ 116th St. - ℘ 212 866 0301 - www. cbccnyc.org - Sunday from 10am.*
First Corinthian Baptist Church – *E2* - *1912 Adam Clayton Blvd. (at 116th St.) Ⓜ 116th St - www.fcbcnyc.org.* Two churches where you can attend a gospel mass on Sunday morning. Spaces limited, arrive early.

BROOKLYN - WILLIAMSBURG

14 **The Knitting Factory** – *E7* - *361 Metropolitan Ave. - Ⓜ Bedford Ave. - ℘ 347 529 6696 - www. knittingfactory.com - 6pm-12am (Fri 3am), Sat 11am-3am, Sun 11am-12am.* Bar and eclectic live music, from acid jazz to rock and electro.
15 **Brooklyn Bowl** – *E7* - *61 Wythe Ave. (At N. 12th St.) - Ⓜ Nassau Ave. - ℘ 718 963 3369 - www. brooklynbowl.com - 👤 - 6pm-12am (Fri 3am), Sat 11am-3am, Sun 11am-12am.* As well as being a pricey bowling alley *($25/30min, shoe rental $5)*, this club hosts themed parties, karaoke, DJs and rock concerts. An eclectic venue offering an original experience.

16 **Union Pool** – *E7* - *484 Union Ave. (at Meeker Ave.) - Ⓜ Lorimer St.- ℘ 718 609 0484 - www.union-pool. com - 4pm-4am, Sat-Sun 2pm-4am.* Both a bar and a live music venue, this Williamsburg staple never goes out of fashion. The large garden decorated with strings of lanterns is another draw; here, you can refuel from El Diablo Tacos food truck.

1 **Music Hall of Williamsburg** – *D7* - *66 N. 6th St. (btw. Kent and Wyth Ave.) - Ⓜ Bedford Ave. - ℘ 718 486 5400 - www.musichallofwilliamsburg. com - opening hours vary depending on shows.* This three-story bar and music venue has a solid rotation of (mostly) indie musical acts and performances.

1 **Nowadays** – *off map* - *56-06 Cooper Ave. #1. (south of Wyckoff Ave.) - Bushwick/Ridgewood - Ⓜ Halsey St. - ℘ 347 523 8535 - nowadays.nyc - Wed-Thur from 5pm, Sat from 12pm, Sun 12-10pm. Closed Mon and Tue.* An indoor/outdoor bar in deep Brooklyn. The sprawling backyard with a ping pong table and picnic benches makes for a chill evening out. Inside, a custom-built sound system and fantastic resident (and visiting) DJs guarantee a solid dance set any night. Absolutely worth the trek.

Café Wha?

Where to stay

This is where the biggest part of your budget will be spent. Don't forget to add taxes (14.25 %) and tips (👌 p. 137). You can reserve flight+ hotel packages through low-cost tour operators (👌 p. 134) or go through **booking centers**: www.booking.com, www.nyc.com. **Hotels** and **Bed & Breakfasts** (www.bbonline.com, www.bedandbreakfast.com) have equivalent rates. If you like going out, go for areas located between Canal and 30th Sts. If you plan to spend much time in Times Square, try Midtown West. Lower Manhattan (Financial District) empties in the evening and is thus fairly quiet.

👌 *Find the addresses on the detachable map (inside the cover) using the numbers in the listing (ex. ①). The coordinates in red (ex. D2) refer to the same map.*

LOWER MANHATTAN

From $240 to $360

㉔ **World Center Hotel** – *A8* - 144 Washington St. - Ⓜ *Cortland St.* - 📞 *212 577 2933 - www.worldcenter hotel.com* - ▤ ✕ - 🅿 *$53 - 169 rooms $189/$329.* Built opposite the World Trade Center (👌 p. 14). Spectacular views over the site and the skyscrapers of Lower Manhattan, especially from the terrace on the 20th floor. Rooms are thoughtfully designed and kitted out with good tech.

CHINATOWN - LITTLE ITALY

Less than $300

⑫ **Best Western Bowery Hanbee** – *B7* - 231 Grand St. - Ⓜ *Grand St.* - 📞 *212 925 1177 - www.bw-bowery hanbeehotel.com* - ▤ - *99 rooms $195/297* ⬤. At the meeting point of Chinatown and Little Italy, this pristine new hotel offers good value for money; small but bright and well put-together rooms.

SOHO

From $230 to $440

⑰ **Hotel Hugo** – *A7* - 525 Greenwich St. - Ⓜ *Spring St.* - 📞 *212 608 4848 - hotelhugony.com* - ▤ - *122 rooms $240/$350.* Tucked away in a quiet corner of Soho, the lobby and rooms of this attractive and discreet hotel are evocative of a luxury ocean liner: Think lacquered wood paneling, clean lines, and elegant décor in darker tones. Superb rooftop (👌 *Azul On The Rooftop, p. 114*).

More than $ 600

⑧ **The Mercer** – *B7* - 147 Mercer St. (at Prince St.) - Ⓜ *Prince St.* - 📞 *212 966 660 - www.mercerhotel.com* - ▤ ✕ - 🅿 *pay* - ♿ - *75 rooms $446/$715.* Artfully decorated mini-lofts, courtesy of French designer Christian Liaigre. Impeccable service. An excellent address with a price to match.

LOWER EAST SIDE

Less than $250

⑬ The Ridge Hotel – *C7* -
*151 E. Houston St. - Ⓜ Lower East
Side/2ⁿᵈ Ave. - ℘ 212 777 0012 -
ridgehotelnyc.com - ▤ - ▣ pay -
♿ - 42 rooms $79/204* ⤴ On a busy
avenue but super central, this is a
modern hotel with slightly cramped
but well-appointed rooms in a great
location.

⑨ Off Soho Suites Hotel – *B7* -
*11 Rivington St. - Ⓜ Bowery - ℘ 212
979 9815 - www.offsoho.com - ▤ ♿ -
38 rooms $165/253.* The name fits—
the hotel is in LES but just off Soho
— and it offers the economical option
to stay in an apartment with a kitchen.

More than $200

① PUBLIC Hotel – *B6* - *215 Chrystie
St. - Ⓜ 2nd Ave. - ℘ 212 735 6000 -
www.publichotels.com - ▤ ✗ -
▣ $40 - 367 rooms $214/$2 000.*
An Ian Schrager concept hotel at
the intersection of the hip Nolita,
Bowery, and LES neighborhoods.
Designed by Herzog & de Meuron,
rooms are contemporary, cozy and
considerably affordable for its brand
and neighborhood. Eat at one of
two Jean-Georges Vongerichten
restaurants or visit the rooftop bar for
panoramic city views.

GREENWICH VILLAGE

From $220 to $250

⑭ Washington Square Hotel – *B6* -
*103 Waverly Pl. - Ⓜ W. 4ᵗʰ St - ℘ 212
777 9515 - washingtonsquarehotel.com*

*- ▤ - ▣ pay - 149 rooms $168/$282 -
✗ dishes $23/$34.* Familial hotel in
Art Deco style, inspired by cinema
photography. Rooms are modestly
sized but very light. Attentive service.

More than $250

① The Marlton Hotel – *B6* - *5 W. 8ᵗʰ
St. - Ⓜ W. 4ᵗʰ St. - ℘ 212 321 0100 -
www.marltonhotel.com - ▤ -
180 rooms $215/$325* ⤴. Rooms
are intimate and charming. As is
the elegent lobby — the fireplace is
especially cozy in colder months.

EAST VILLAGE

Less than $200

⑮ St. Mark's Hotel – *C6* - *2 St. Mark's
Pl. - Ⓜ Astor Pl. - ℘ 212 674 0100 -
www.stmarkshotel.net - ▤ -
64 rooms $100/$140.* The comforts
are basic, there are single beds
and it's quite noisy, but it is well
maintained. Ideally located for heavy
sleepers who like going out at night.
No elevator.

129

More than $300

② The Bowery Hotel – *C7* - *335
Bowery - Ⓜ Bleecker St. - ℘ 212 505
9100 - www.theboweryhotel.com -
▤ ✗ - ▣ pay - ♿ - 135 rooms. $365/
$575.* The charm of Old Europe is in
evidence in this establishment. Some
rooms have a private terrace with a
view over the city. Very good Italian
food in the hotel restaurant.

CHELSEA - MEATPACKING

From $145 to $375

16 **Chelsea Savoy** – *B5* - *204 W. 23rd St.* - Ⓜ *23rd St.* - ☎ *212 929 9353* - *www.chelseasavoy.com* - 🖥 ♿ - *98 rooms $125/225.* Located near public transportation, this is a comfortable hotel; it is quite impersonal but well-equipped. The rooms on the first floor street side can be noisy.

☺ **27** **Fairfield Inn & Suites Chelsea** – *C5* - *116 West 28th St. (at 6th Ave.)* - Ⓜ *28th St.* - ☎ *212 206 0998* - *fairfield.marriott.com* - 🖥 - 🅿 *$39/$49* - ♿ - *110 rooms $112/$368* 🍽. An excellent hotel, which is particularly well situated. It's hard to fault. The welcome is warm and efficient, the rooms are decently sized, clean and demurely (but elegantly) decorated, with wood furnishings. The breakfast is generous. Recommended.

130

MADISON SQUARE

Less than $350

18 **Clarion Hotel Park Avenue** – *C5* - *429 Park Ave. S.* - Ⓜ *28th St.* - ☎ *212 532 4860* - *www.clarionpark.com* - 🖥 - 🅿 *Pay*- *60 rooms $109/$274.* Though they are a little impersonal, the rooms are light and pleasant. Those facing the back of the hotel are quieter but a bit dark.

4 **The Evelyn** – *C5* - *7 East 27th St. (btw Madison and 5th Aves.)* - Ⓜ *28th St.* - ☎ *212 545 8000* - *www. theevelyn.com* - ✗ - 🅿 *Pay* - ♿ - *wifi* -

170 rooms $138/$332. The flamboyantly decorated facade and colorful décor are the big draws of this hotel, which attracts young artists and fashion professionals.

MIDTOWN WEST

Less than $250

20 **The Hotel @ Times Square** – *C5* - *59 W. 46th St.* - Ⓜ *47-50 Sts. Rockefeller Center* - ☎ *212 790 2710* - *www.hoteltsq.com* - 🖥 - 🅿 *$27/37* - *213 rooms $111/$232* 🍽. Steps from Times Square but not too noisy. Renovated in light and functional style. Well-equipped rooms.

5 **Hudson New York** – *C4* - *358 West 58th St.* - Ⓜ *Columbus Circle* - ☎ *212 554 6000* - *www.hudsonhotel. com* - 🖥 ✗ ♿ - *866 rooms $93/$220.* The interiors of this former boarding school, renovated by Philippe Starck, present a whirlwind of grandeur and eclecticism. Very pleasant terrace with a view over Central Park. The modest size of the rooms is compensated for by attractive deals on the hotel's website.

From $240 to $360

19 **414 Hotel** – *C4* - *414 W. 46th St. (near 9th Ave.)* - Ⓜ *50th St.* - ☎ *212 399 0006* - *www.414hotel.com* - 🖥 ✗ - *22 rooms $249/$340* 🍽. Set in the quiet of a tree-lined road, this hotel is housed across two brick houses joined by a pretty patio. The rooms are a little small and soberly decorated in a very New York style. The overall effect is a relaxing atmosphere with the feel of a family hotel.

21 Belvedere – *C4* - *319 W. 48th St.
- 🚇 50th St. - ☎ 212 245 7000 -
www.belvederehotelnyc.com - 🍽 ✕ -
🅿 pay - ♿ - 400 rooms $229/$323.*
A little removed from the activity of
Times Square, a beautiful hotel in the
great tradition of New York Art Deco.
Elegant and spacious rooms, which
enjoy lots of natural light at the front
of the hotel, equipped with all the best
comforts. Impeccable service.

More than $350

1 The Knickerbocker – *C5* -
*6 Broadway (at W. 42nd St.) - 🚇 Times
Square-42nd St. - ☎ 212 204 4980 -
theknickerbocker.com - 🍽 ✕
- 330 rooms $340/$650.* A luxe oasis
right in the heart of Times Square,
this historic 1906 building got a 2015
facelift, but still retains plenty of
old New York charm. Eat at Charlie
Palmer's restaurant or go all out for
New Year's Eve on St. Cloud rooftop.

MIDTOWN EAST

Less than $250

1 The Gregory – *C5* - *42 W. 35th
S. - 🚇 34th St.-Herald Sq. - ☎ 212 947
0200 - www.thegregoryhotelnewyork.
com - 🍽 ✕ - 🅿 $42 - ♿ - 132 rooms.
$110/$280* 🚆 Right by Macy's
(👤 p.122) and minutes from the
Empire State Building (👤 p.54), this
handsome hotel is a welcome addition
to the neighborhood, especially for its
affordable price point.

More than $250

1 1 Hotel Central Park – *CD4* -
*1414 6th Ave. (at W. 58th St.) - 🚇 57th
St. - ☎ 212 703 2001 - www.1hotels.*

*com/central-park - 🍽 ✕ - 🅿 - ♿ -
229 rooms. $318/ $1 300.* A focus on
sustainability without compromising
on design. Modern rooms are outfitted
with reclaimed wood and industrial-
style windows. Great service. Ask for a
room with a Park view.

😊 6 Library Hotel – *C5* - *299
Madison Ave. - 🚇 Grand Central Term. -
☎ 212 983 4500 - www.libraryhotel.
com - 🍽 ♿ - 60 rooms $223/$447*
🚆. Elegant, welcoming and quiet, and
filled with books (more than 6 000!).
Design décor and superb terrace.

UPPER WEST SIDE

From $200 to $360

23 Hotel Belleclaire – *C3* - *250 W.
77th St. - 🚇 79th St. - ☎ 212 362 7700 -
www.hotelbelleclaire.com - 🍽 -
🅿 $51 - ♿ - 244 rooms $210/$365.*
Close to Central Park and Lincoln
Center, in a residential neighborhood.
Expect simple, well-maintained rooms
with understated décor, all equipped
with a refrigerator. Good value.

UPPER EAST SIDE

From $375

😊 25 Loews Regency – *D4* -
*540 Park Ave. - 🚇 Lexington Ave. -
☎ 212 759 4100 - www.loewshotels.
com - 🍽 ✕ - 🅿 $80 - ♿ - 379 rooms
and 58 suites $329/$1 169* 🚆. Light
and spacious rooms decorated
simply mixing light colors and
contemporary touches. Friendly and
effective service. One of the best in
its category, close to Central Park, the
Met and the subway.

Planning Your Trip

Know before you go

Williamsburg Bridge and Downtown Manhattan
© T. Shi Photography/Moment/Getty Images

Know before you go

ENTRY REQUIREMENTS

ID – To enter the United States without a visa, you will need a **biometric** passport issued after 26 October **2006**. In all other cases, obtaining a visa is obligatory. If in doubt, consult the website of the American Embassy**.**

Visa – If you have a valid passport and are travelling for business or leisure for **less than three months**, a visa is not necessary. If your trip does not fit this criteria, a visa is obligatory and if it is likely you will exercise a professional activity during your stay.

ESTA (Electronic System for Travel Authorization) – Since January 2009, it has been obligatory for travellers without visas to fill in, at least 72 hours before departure, an **electronic questionnaire** (health, criminal record, etc.) available on embassy website.

Customs– Arms, drugs, vegetable products and food products and some kinds of medications are forbidden on American soil. The following are permitted: 1 l of alcohol (for over 21s), 200 cigarettes, 50 cigars or 2 kg of tobacco. Gifts must represent a sum of less than $100 (keep your receipts).

Other elements to provide – A **return ticket**, plane or boat, and the **address** of where you're staying. Without these you risk being turned back. Electronic devices must not be out of battery.

GETTING TO NEW YORK

♿ To find out more about **airports**, go to *Getting to New York, p. 3*.

The main providers

Air France – ☏ 36 54 (€ 0.35/min) - www.airfrance.fr.
American Airlines – ☏ 0 821 980 999 (€ 0.12/min) - www.americanairlines.fr.
Delta Airlines – ☏ 0892 702 609 - www.delta.com.
Icelandair – ☏ 01 44 51 60 51 - www.icelandair.fr.
KLM – ☏ 09 69 36 86 05 (reservations) - www.klm.com.

Low-cost agencies

Travel agents compare prices and offer flight bookings or package deals. Here is a selection:
E-Dreams – www.edreams.fr
Easy Vols – www.easyvols.fr
Expedia – www.expedia.fr

MONEY

The **dollar** ($) is divided into 100 **cents**. You'll find bills of 1, 5, 10, 50 and 100 dollars, and coins of 1, 5, 10, 25 and 50 cents. A dime is worth 10 cents, a quarter 25 cents.
Exchange rate: around $1 for £0.77 (January 2020).
Credit cards – Accepted, without a limit for payments. The exchange rate is made on the day of the transaction, with a commission added.

Cash points /ATMs – Available throughout the city, they apply the exchange rate at the time of the transaction, and a flat commission is taken. It is better value to take out a large sum.

HEALTH INSURANCE

Do not scrimp on health insurance, as fees can rise very high and very quickly indeed. Tour operators generally propose a very comprehensive insurance policy. Check with your bank whether international coverage is included with your bank card. Work out exactly what the steps to follow are in the case of an accident, and which forms you need to fill out.

SEASONS

New York has a temperate continental climate, which is fairly humid and characterised with a wide temperature range.

Summer – The average temperature hovers at around 30 °C in the day, and a little below 20 °C at night

Winter – Cold and humid with some fine sunny days. In December to February, temperatures can fall to under 0 °C? The winter is only really harsh when there are blizzards, accompanied by snow. Celebrate Christmas and New Year at Times Square.

Spring and autumn – Mild, between 15 and 25 °C. The transition of May-June is one of the most pleasant times of year. The autumn, in the glow of Indian summer, is the start of the

© J. D. Price/Moment/Getty Images

Times Square in snow

cultural season, a time for shopping and for celebrations (Halloween, Thanksgiving).

Precipitation – Throughout the year; bring an umbrella.

INFORMATION

Websites

City of New York – www.nyc.gov
Restaurants, cultural agendas – www.timeoutny.com
nymag.com
www.nytimes.com
www.villagevoice.com

Tourist office

Tourist office – www.nycgo.com
Official NYC Information Center: 151 W. 34th St. - Mon-Fri 10am-10pm, Sat 10am-7pm, Sun 11am-7pm.

Basic information

BANKS

There are banks and ATMs on practically every corner. Unless you use your own bank, expect to pay a fee of $2.50-4. *◔ Money, p. 134 and Opening hours, facing page.*

BIKES

Traffic in New York can be crazy. Unless you have experience with urban cycling, you should cycle only in parks and protected bike lanes. There are many shops that rent bikes. New York's bike share program is called **Citi Bike**, and there are docks everywhere. $12/24 hours (unlimited 30min rides). **www.citibikenyc.com**.

IKEA shuttle

BOATS

Ferry

East River The ferry plies the East River, stopping in Manhattan, Brooklyn, Queens, and Governor's Island (seasonal). $2.75/single ride (free transfer available). Expect lines. *www.ferry.nyc*

IKEA – IKEA run a ferry between Pier 11/Wall St. and Red Hook. $5 on weekdays (but free with purchase of at least $10). Free on weekends. Free for under 12. Expect lines.

Hop-on/Hop-off $35 ($15 online), valid for a day for unlimited journeys. *℘ 212 445-7599 - www.citysightseeingnewyork.com*

Staten Island - The ferry (free, 24hr/day) leaves from South Ferry in Battery Park (*◔ p. 25*). Good view of Statue of Liberty.

CONSULATES

Consulate of Canada – 466 Lexington Ave., 20th flr. - *℘ 844 880 6519 - www.international.gc.ca/ - Mon-Fri 9am-5pm.*

British Consulate – 885 2nd Ave. - *℘ 212 745 0200 - www.gov.uk - Mon-Fri 9am-4pm* (by appointment only unless emergency).

Australian Consulate – 150 E. 42nd St., 34th flr. - *℘ 212 351 6500- usa. embassy.gov.au/new-york - Mon-Fri 9am-5pm.*

© Y. Kanazawa/Michelin

EATING OUT

You can eat at all hours in New York: the local routine is a hearty breakfast from 7am, a light lunch on the go, with dinner remaining the most important meal of the day (until 11pm). On weekends, **brunch** serves as breakfast and lunch (between 10am and 4pm). Options in New York include street stands and food trucks (under $8) food from around the world (less than $12 in small shops), and restaurants for varying budgets. There are special deals (*Early Bird* or the *Pre-Theater Menu*) served in the early evening, between 5pm and 7pm or 7.30pm: with these, you can get dinner for less than $30. **Drinks** at restaurants are expensive, particularly wine, which is served by the glass ($8 to $15). Some restaurants are BYOB. Tax (8.875 %) and tip (15-20%) are not included in listed prices

Many **grocery stores** have a prepared foods section, offering salads and hot dishes. 👌 *Tips p. 141 and Addresses/ Where to eat, p. 104.*

ELECTRICITY

American plug sockets are different to British plugs. Bring an adapter from home. The current here is 110V.

INTERNET

Many cafés, some bars and most hotels offer free WiFi. There is also the possibility of network access in public parks. LinkNYC kiosks on the street provide free WiFi and charging ports.

OPENING HOURS

Shops – Mon-Sat 10am-7 or 8pm. Many shops do stay open until 9 or 10pm. Everything is open Sundays but usually at 11am. Many convenience stores and pharmacies are open 24/7.

Banks – Mon-Fri 9am-3.30pm, sometimes Sat 9am-12pm.

Pharmacies – Duane Reade, Walgreens, and CVS are everywhere, and many are open 24/7.

Post Office – Mon-Fri 8.30am-5pm or 6pm, Sat morning, opening hours vary. The Central Post Office (441-445 8th Ave.) is open 24hr/day.

PRESS

Newspapers – *New York Times* (paper of record), *New York Post, New York Daily News* (tabloids).

Magazines – *Time Out New York* and *New York Magazine* are weekly magazines that cover cultural outings and the city's latest hot spots. *The New Yorker* is known for the quality of its writing and sophistication of its criticism.

POST

Price of a stamp: $ 1.15 for a postcard or letter (28g/1oz maximum). Allow a week for delivery to Europe.

PUBLIC HOLIDAYS

New Year's Day: January 1.
Martin Luther King Jr.'s Birthday: 3rd Monday of January.
President's Day: 3rd Monday of February.
Memorial Day: Last Monday of May.
Independence Day: July 4.
Labor Day: 1st Monday of September.
Columbus Day: 2nd Monday of October.
Veterans Day: November 11.
Thanksgiving Day: Last Thursday of November.
Christmas Day: December 25.

PUBLIC TRANSPORT

Public transport is the most economical and often fastest way to get around New York. The transport network—bus, subway and regional trains— is administered by the MTA (Metropolitan Transportation Authority): **www.mta.info**. Free maps in stations and online.

♧ Subway map on the back of the detachable map.

Subway

Tickets and prices– A single ride ticket ($2.75) is valid for one journey including transfers to other subway lines but not to the bus.
The pay-per-ride **MetroCard** can be charged from $5.50 to $80. A new MetroCard itself costs $1. You can transfer between bus and subway once (within 2hrs of swiping). Refill the card as many times as you like (5% bonus each time you charge $5.50 or more. It can swiped a maximum of four times in a row.
Unlimited Ride MetroCard: 7-Day ($33) and 30-day ($127): unlimited access to metro and bus.
Getting around in the metro – Lines have a number or a letter. When identifying which platform to take, it's either the **direction** that counts (Downtown, Uptown) or the **destination** (Brooklyn, Queens, Manhattan). Look closely at the signs. In some stations, there is a separate entrance for each direction, and once you have passed through with your ticket, it will no longer be valid in the other direction if you make a mistake. Some lines are local, others express: an announcement will say what kind of train it is before the train arrives. Several lines, such as the C and E, 2 and 3, or 4 and 5, use the same platform, look closely at the **number** or **letter** displayed on the front of the train and on the side of the car. If you have an unlimited ride card and you exit the subway station, you'll have to wait 18min before you can use your card again.
Subways run **24hr/day**, every 2 to 5min at rush hour (7.30am-9am, 5pm-6.30pm) and up to 20min between 12am and 6.30am. Some stations are closed at night.
Safety – The subway is safe but, as with any big city, some care and caution is advised. Note that if a subway car is empty, there is a reason and it should be avoided.

Subway trains in Queens

Bus

The pricing system is the same as for the subway. MetroCards can also be used on the buses. Lines are distinguished by a **number**. The preceding letter indicates the corresponding borough: M for Manhattan, B for Brooklyn, Bx for Bronx, Q for Queens. In Manhattan, the cross-town buses have the numbers of the streets on which they drive (ex. M34 = 34th St). To ask for the next stop (every two or three blocks), press the red "Stop" buttons or the vertical yellow strips between the windows. Many lines run **24hr/day** (less frequent at night). Between 8pm and 5am, you can ask the driver to let you off anywhere on the route.

Transfers – If you have a pay-per-ride MetroCard, changes from bus to metro or one bus to another are included in your ticket for 2 hours after first using it. If you have an Unlimited Ride MetroCard, changes are unlimited. If you are paying with cash, transfers are only free for bus lines that intersect with the one you have taken. To use cash, you need exact change in coins only (no bills).
♿ Getting to New York p. 3.

SIGHTSEEING

Most museums are closed Mondays and on the main public holidays. Tickets are expensive, but the museums have set times where entry is free.

Various **passes** offer entry to a selection of museums and tourist sites for a flat rate. Pamphlets are available in tourist offices, hotels and online.

The **City Pass** offers the best deal. It is valid for nine days and costs $132 for an adult, $108 for a child aged between 6 and 17. It includes access to the Empire State Building, the Metropolitan Museum of Art and the American Museum of Natural History, as well as 3 other attractions chosen from: the Guggenheim, Top of the Rock, the Statue of Liberty, the Circle Line cruise, 9/11 Memorial & Museum or Intrepid Sea, Air & Space Museum. See *www.citypass.com*.

The **New York Pass** exists in 1-day ($134), 2-day ($199), 3-day ($274), 4-day ($299), 5-day ($329) and 7-day ($379) versions. Cheaper online: *www.newyorkpass.com*. Calculate carefully what is viable, because it is impossible to see everything in the time given. It gives entry, among others, to a cruise around Manhattan, to the Empire State Building, the Museum of Natural History and many themed routes, guided tours and attractions, as well as the major museums (MoMA, Guggenheim, the Met, the Whitney, but not the Frick). Reductions in shops and restaurants, and for Broadway shows. It is particularly suited to families with children.

TAXES

Prices are always given without tax (including in this guide). Tax + tips inflate the bill by 25-30 %. Tax in hotels is 14.75 %. For restaurants and all other products and services (décor, bike hire, etc.), it is 8.875 %. Clothing under $110 is not taxed. There is no tax on groceries, diapers, newspapers and magazines, laundry services, and a few other things.

TAXI

Initial charge – $2.50.

Meter – $0.50 per 0.5 miles or per min. stopped or significantly slowed down.

Rush hour – Mon-Fri 4pm-8pm, $1/journey supplement.

Night – 8pm-6am, supplement $0.50/journey.

City tax – $0.50/journey.

Tip – $1 (not obligatory but strongly recommended).

Maximum number of passengers: 4 unless in a van.

Taxis are available if their roof light (with number) is on.

The website **www.taxifarefinder.com** gives you a price estimation for your journey. ♿ *Getting to New York, p. 3.*

CAR SERVICES

There are several app-based car services in NYC: **Lyft**, **Via**, and **Uber**. Pricing is usually similar. These are almost always less expensive than a taxi, especially if you choose a shared ride. During rush hour, a taxi to the airport will usually cost less than a car service because it is a flat rate.

TIME DIFFERENCE

New York is on Eastern Standard Time (EST), **5hrs** behind **London**. The change to **summer time** takes place in Mar., and to **winter time** in Nov.

TELEPHONE

From overseas to New York

To call New York, dial 1, followed by the area code, and the 7 figures of the number of the person you're calling. For Manhattan, the area code is 212, 646 or 917. For the other boroughs (Brooklyn, Bronx, Queens and Staten Island), it's 718. Numbers preceded by 800 or 1-800 are *toll-free* inside the United States. It is now possible to use them from abroad by replacing them by 880 or 881.

From New York to overseas

To call Europe, dial 011 followed by the country code (UK 44), then the number of the person you're calling minus the first '0'.

From New York to New York

Dial the area code directly followed by the 7 figures of the number of the person you're calling. Information : 411 (free call in phone booths).

Mobile phones – Your phone must be 3G- or 4G-enabled to work. Before your trip, contact your provider to find out the rates for the US. You can buy an American SIM card at local provider shops (like T-Mobile), and also in most convenience stores and corner shops. These cards usually include a certain number of calls, SMS and data; sometimes calls and SMS are unlimited.

TIPS

Except when service is included (which is not very common), it is customary to leave between 15%

and 20% of the bill. In a hotel, $1 to a porter (for 1-2 bags), and *at least* $3 daily for housekeeping.

TOBACCO

Smoking is not allowed in public transport, offices, hotels, taxis, restaurants or bars. It is generally allowed only in some parks and on the street.
Cigarettes are expensive and can be bought in drug stores, corner stores and kiosks. Prices vary.

TOILETS

There are not many public toilets *(rest rooms)*. You will find them in parks. Starbucks is popular for its toilets.

TOURS

There are a plethora of options on offer, consult: **www.nycgo.com**, which lists them.

By foot

Big Apple Greeter – www.bigapple greeter.org. To discover the city from inside with volunteering New Yorkers (get in touch 2-3 weeks before). Free, but tips welcome.

Greenwich Village Literary Pub Crawl – ☏ 917 865 4575 - literarypubcrawl. com - Saturdays. Meet at 12pm inside White Horse Tavern, 567 Hudson St. - $35 (seniors and students above 21 years $30). Head off on the trail of famous actors (Jack Kerouac) and abstract expressionist painters (Jackson Pollock), and drink in the bars that they frequented.

Joyce Gold – ☏ 212 242 5762 - joycegoldhistorytours.com - $25 per person. Historical routes; timetable on website.

Urban Oyster Tour – ☏ 347 618 8687 - www.urbanoyster.com - from $79 (tastings included) for tours of about 3hrs. Interesting themed visits around food and drink.

Big Onion Tours – ☏ 212 439 1090 - www.bigonion.com - from $25 (seniors and students $20) - Advanced booking required for some tours. Experienced educators and history graduate students take guests on historic tours around different themes or neighborhoods.

Bus, boat, helicopter

Circle Line Cruises – ☏ 212 563 3200 - www.circleline.com. Mini-cruises around Manhattan on river boat. From $18-69 (3-12 years $18-62) depending on length of tour from 1hr to 2hr30min.

Hop-on/Hop-off $59 ($39 online), valid for a day for unlimited journeys. ☏ 212 445-7599 - www.citysightseeingnewyork.com

On Location Tours – ☏ 212 683 2027 - onlocationtours.com/new-york-tours - from $31 to $62. TV fans will love these bus journeys around the filming locations and memorable sites from the series.

Liberty Helicopters – ☏ 800 542 9933 - www.libertyhelicopters. com - from $180 (around 15min flight time). See New York from a bird's-eye view. Note that this company has had several fatal crashes.

Bryant Park

Festivals and events

ANNUAL EVENTS

January

▶ **The Winter Show** – Park Avenue Armory (at 67th St. and Park Ave.) - End January - thewintershow.org.

▶ **NYC Restaurant Week® Winter** – Modestly priced menus in well-reputed restaurants. There is also a summer edition. - Jan to Feb - nycgo. com/restaurantweek.

February

▶ **Lunar New Year Festival and Parade** – Chinatown (in either Jan or Feb, depends on lunar calendar).

▶ **Black History Month** – Events around the theme of black identity.

▶ **Westminster Dog Show** – Madison Square Garden - www.westminsterkennelclub.org.

March

▶ **The Armory Show** – Large contemporary art fair at Pier 94 - www.thearmoryshow.com.

▶ **St Patrick's Day** – parade on 5th Avenue - March 17.

▶ **Macy's Spring Flower Show** – Thousands of flowers are displayed in the Macy's windows for two weeks in late March.

▶ **New Directors/New Film** – Lincoln Center and MoMA, 10 days in late March to discover rising filmmakers from around the world.

▶ **Easter Sunday Parade** – Parade on 5th Avenue - Easter Sunday.

April

▶ **Spring Flower Exhibition** – , New York Botanical Garden - from mid-April until June.

▶ **Tribeca Film Festival** – Independent film festival (👍 *p. 32*) - late April - tribecafilm.com/festival.

▶ **Central Brooklyn Jazz Festival** – Jazz concerts from mid-April to mid-May - centralbrooklynjazz.org.

▶ **Art Expo New York** – Pier 94 on the Hudson River - mid-late April - www.artexponewyork.com.

▶ **Cherry Blossom Festival** – Brooklyn Botanic Garden (👍 *p. 96*) - late April-early May - bbg.org.

May

▶ **Empire State Building Run-Up** – Race up the stairs of the skyscraper.

▶ **Five Boro Bike Tour** – 67km/41mi of bike route around the five boroughs - 1st Sunday of May. - www.bike.nyc.

▶ **Memorial Day Parades** – Parades in all areas in memory of military personnel who died in service - 4th Monday of May.

▶ **Washington Square Outdoor Art Exhibit** – Memorial Day wknd.-Washington Square. There is also an autumn edition. - www.wsoae.org.

June

▶ **Museum Mile Festival** – Festival of Upper East Side museums - 2nd Tues. of June - museummilefestival.org.

▶ **Puerto Rican Day Parade** – on 5th Avenue - 2nd Sun of June.

▶**NY Philharmonic Parks Concerts** – Free concerts in different parks - mid-June - www.nycgovparks.org.

▶**Mermaid Parade** – At Coney Island - mid June, a colorful mermaid parade - www.coneyisland.com.

▶**Pride Week** – Parade along 5th Avenue - Last Sunday of June.

▶**SummerStage** – Various open-air shows and concerts, most free - June through Oct. - www.cityparksfoundation.org.

▶**Midsummer Night's Swing** – Concerts and dance shows on the plaza of the Lincoln Center - end June-mid July - www.lincolncenter.org/midsummer-night-swing.

July - August

▶**Independence Day** – National Day: 4 July, fireworks on the Hudson and the East River and boat parade at South Street Seaport.

▶**Shakespeare in the Park** – Open-air in Central Park - July-Aug - publictheater.org/programs/shakespeare-in-the-park.

▶**Mostly Mozart Festival** – Concerts at the Lincoln Center - July-Aug - www.lincolncenter.org/mostly-mozart-festival.

▶**Lincoln Center Out of Doors** – Free concerts and ballet held in the open air - end July - lcoutofdoors.org.

▶**NYC Restaurant Week® Summer** – Modestly priced menus in well-reputed restaurants - end of July to mid-Aug - nycgo.com/restaurantweek.

▶**US Open** – Flushing Meadows - end Aug-mid Sept - www.usopen.org.

© Beboy_ltd/iStock

Independence Day fireworks over the Hudson

▶**Summer on the Hudson** – Free concerts and activites in Riverside Park - May-Sept.

▶**Celebrate Brooklyn** – Free concerts, film screenings and music in Prospect Park - June-Aug - www.bricartsmedia.org.

▶**Summer Streets** – 7 miles of NYC streets open to the public to play, run, walk, bike - three Sundays in Aug.

September

▶**Labor Day** – first Mon in Sept.

▶**Brazilian Parade** on Avenue of the Americas (6th Ave.) and **West Indian Day Parade** - first Mon in Sept.

▶**NYC Century Ride** – 55, 75 or 100mi bike ride around NYC - early Sept - nyccentury.org.
▶**Feast of San Gennaro** – Italian festival in Little Italy - mid-Sept.
▶**BAM Next Wave Festival** – Experimental dance, concerts and theatre at Brooklyn Academy of Music - mid-Sept to mid-Dec - www.bam.org.
▶**New York Film Festival** – Lincoln Center - until mid Oct - www.filmlinc.org.

October
▶**Open House New York** – Free tours to many historic, usually private, buildings around the city - two wknds. in mid Oct - ohny.org.
▶**New York Comic Con** – Jacob K. Javits Convention Center - early Oct - www.newyorkcomiccon.com.
▶**Village Halloween Parade** – Legendary celebration of Halloween - October 31.

November
▶**New York City Marathon** – first Sun. in Nov.
▶**Veterans Day Parade** – 5th Avenue - 11 Nov - parade.uwvc.org
▶**Macy's Thanksgiving Day Parade** – Along Broadway from Central Park to Herald Square - 4th Thurs in Nov.
▶**Holiday Train Show** – Grand Central Terminal and New York Botanical Garden - through Jan/Feb.

December
▶**Tree-Lighting** – Turning on the Christmas lights, particularly at Rockefeller Center and the corner of 5th Ave./59th St., near Central Park - from December 4.

▶**First Night Festival** – Fireworks in Central Park and South Street Seaport - December 31 - **New Year's Eve Ball Drop** is the big gathering on Times Square, before midnight, where the crowd rings in the New Year as the famous "ball" drops down the *Times building*. It is followed by the **Midnight Run** in Central Park.

BIENNALE

Whitney Biennial – At the Whitney Museum of American Art, you'll find the trends of contemporary art. The biennial is three months every spring. - whitney.org/biennial.

BIG EXHIBITIONS

Museums – New York's big museums, such as MoMA (♻ *p. 58*), the Met (♻ *p. 74*), the Whitney (♻ *p. 71*), the Museum of Natural History (♻ *p. 86*) and the Guggenheim (♻ *p. 80*) have major exhibitions all year round. See their websites for calendars.

Things to do in NYC
New York also has many **free papers** and **magazines** *(some below are not free)* with cultural agendas and listings. See *City Guide Magazine* (www.cityguideny.com); *In New York* (www.innewyork.com); *The Skint* (www.theskint.com; *Time Out New York* (www.timeout.com/newyork); *New York* magazine (nymag.com); and the *New Yorker* (www.newyorker.com).

Find Out More

Hudson Street, Greenwich Village
© O. Korshakov/Moment/Getty Images

Key dates

1524 - Giovanni da Verrazzano, sent by French king François I, discovers the site of New York.

1609 - Henry Hudson, with the Dutch West India Company explores the river that now takes his name.

1614 - The region becomes a Dutch colony: New Netherland.

1625 - A trading post called New Amsterdam is established at the bottom tip of Manhattan.

1626 - Peter Minuit "buys" Manhattan from the Algonquins.

1636 - Dane Johannes Bronck established a homestead in the area that would become the Bronx.

1644 - Slaves brought by the Dutch in 1626 were freed.

1647 - **Peter Stuyvesant** becomes director-general of the colony.

1653 - He orders the construction of a fortified wall in the location of today's Wall Street.

1657 - Arrival of the English Quakers.

1664 - New Amsterdam is taken by the English and becomes New York.

1667 - Treaty of Breda gives English possession of the colony.

1673 - Holland takes back the city, naming it New Orange.

1674 - Treaty of Westminster returns New Netherland to England.

1725 - William Bradford creates the city's first newspaper, the *New York Gazette*.

1763 - The Treaty of Paris confirms England's domination on the North American continent.

1764-1765 - The Sugar Act and the Stamp Act provoke agitation against the English, leading to the union of nine colonies.

1767 - The "Townsend Taxes" imposed heavily on the colonies cause uproar.

4 July 1767 - Adoption of the **Declaration of Independence**.

1783 - The Treaty of Paris recognizes the independence of the thirteen American colonies. **George Washington** enters triumphantly into New York, which would become the following year the first capital of the United States.

1789 - Washington is elected first president of the United States.

1807 - Fulton links New York to Albany with his steamboat.

1811 - John Randel Jr's plan divides the city into a grid following 12 longitudinal avenues and 155 crossing horizontal roads.

1812 - The US declares war against Great Britain. New York is affected by the blockade.

1817 - Creation of the Stock Exchange (⚓ *p. 156*).

1820 - New York is the biggest city in the country (123 706 habitants).

1825 - The Erie Canal links the Great Lakes to the port of New York, which quickly swallows up half the imports for the whole of the United States.

1827 - **Slavery** is abolished in the state of New York.

1835 - A fire ravishes the city.

1845 - The first telegraphic line links New York to Philadelphia.

1851 - Publication of *New York Times*.

1857 - Construction of Central Park begins (♿ *p. 67*).

1861-1865 - American Civil War. Display of the body of **Lincoln** at City Hall after his assassination.

1868 - First overground subway.

1869 - Black Friday and city taken by financial panic.

1872 - Inauguration of the Metropolitan Museum of Art (♿ *p. 74*).

1886 - Inauguration of the **Statue of Liberty** (♿ *p. 22*).

1891 - Inauguration of Carnegie Hall (♿ *p. 52*).

1902 - Completion of Flatiron Building (♿ *p. 49*).

1904 - First underground subway line.

1913 - Duchamp creates a scandal at the first modern art exhibition, the New York Armory Show.

1917-1919 - The US take part in WWI.

1919-1933 - Prohibition of alcohol.

1929 - Wall Street Crash.

1931 - Inauguration of the Empire State Building (♿ *p. 54*).

1939 - Inauguration of Rockefeller Center (♿ *p. 57*).

1941-1945 - The US take part in WWII.

1952 - UN headquarters established in New York.

1965 - Assassination of civil rights activist Malcolm X in Harlem.

1970 - First New York City Marathon.

1973 - Inauguration of the World Trade Center (♿ *p. 14*).

1993 - Explosion of a terrorist bomb at the World Trade Center.

1994 - Rudolph Giuliani becomes mayor.

Jan 2001 - Hillary Clinton starts her term as US Senator from New York.

11 Sept 2001 - Terrorist attack and destruction of the World Trade Center: 2,752 dead and missing.

4 July 2004 - First stone of Freedom Tower laid, renamed One World Trade Center.

Sept 2008 - Fall of Lehman Brothers and financial crisis. Wall Street collapses.

Nov 2008 - Barack Obama is elected president of the United States.

Jan 2010 - Michael Bloomberg, elected for the first time in 2002, starts his third mandate as mayor.

2012 - One World Trade Center becomes the highest tower in New York (541m/17,775ft).

Oct 2012 - Hurricane Sandy hits New York, leading to 41 deaths and causing $40bn. of damage. The 43rd New York City Marathon is canceled.

151

Nov 2012 - Barack Obama re-elected President of the United States.

Nov 2013 - Democrat Bill de Blasio elected as mayor.

Nov 2016 - Hillary Clinton takes 48% of the popular vote, but Donald Trump is nonetheless elected President of the United States.

Oct 2017 - New York commits to upholding Paris Agreement principles.

21 Jan 2017 - More than 400,000 protestors marched in New York's Women's March.

Nov 2017 - New York commits to being a sanctuary city for immigrants and refugees.

Nov 2017 - NYC Mayor Bill de Blasio re-elected for second term.

Sept 2019 - Central Park Tower tops out at 1,550 ft (472m), making it the world's tallest residential building.

The Big Apple

A LAND TO CONQUER

Giovanni da Verrazzano, a Florentine explorer serving the French king François I, arrived at the bay of New York in 1524. He baptised the area the "Terre d'Angoulême" (land of Angoulême, a commune in southwestern France) in honor of his feudal overlord from the family of des Valois Angoulême. In 1609, Englishman **Henry Hudson**, a navigator exploring on behalf of the Dutch, would also come to the region. Sailing the river that today carries his name, he encountered Amerindians and left decreeing these territories Dutch property. The traders entered into negotiation with the "Indians" (Native Americans), comprising two groups: the Mohawks from the Iroquois Confederacy, and the Algonquin people, also called "Delaware".

NEW AMSTERDAM

In 1614, Dutch West India Company founded the **colony of New Netherland**, on the site of present-day New York. In 1626, **Peter Minuit** bought Manhattan (from the Algonquin word, *menatay*, meaning "island") from the Wappingers for 60 florins (or just $26!). Racial tensions were created under the pressure of the colonists. The first violence occurred in 1640, against the Algonquins. Subsequently, with each changing alliance, the different Amerindian tribes of the region would participate in the wars between rival settlers.

BIRTH OF A CITY

After constructing fortifications on the southern tip of the island of Manhattan, Dutch engineer **Fredericksz** developed the plans for the future city, New Amsterdam. He would design winding roads with *boweries* (farms) built either side, on often swampy land; the Dutch ancestral experience of drainage worked wonders. Agricultural areas would appear further to the north and in the areas of Brooklyn, Queens, the Bronx and Staten Island. But the great urban construction project was never fully finished. Only the defensive wall would be significant enough that the road that replaced it retained the name, Wall Street. The famous **Peter Stuyvesant** would be the last director-general of this colony. Holland decided to concentrate on Asia, and New Netherland was practically abandoned. In 1664, the town was given to the English without a fight, who would rule over it for 119 years. New Amsterdam was renamed "New York" in honor of the brother of King Charles II, the Duke of York.

Immigration

Attracted by its seemingly limitless development, immigrants started arriving in New York, with new waves coming across as successive wars, political conflicts and economic troubles hit Europe.

THE IRISH WAVE

In 1860, Irish people represented a third of the city's inhabitants. Poor and often illiterate, they were held in disdain by the descendants of the settlers and had to fight to survive. The first known gangs of New York were Irish (see 2002 film *Gangs of New York*). Over time they gained power over the city police. These gangs, which were soon joined by immigrants of other origins — Italian, Jewish, Central American, South American and Asian — would be one of the dominating factors of the life of the city, across every time period.

BLACK HISTORY OF NEW YORK

Less known is the story of the immigration of black people, of which the history is troubled and somewhat murky. In 1626, the Dutch brought enslaved people from Africa, as the English would do later. Several slave markets would prosper on Wall Street. In 1827, the slave trade was officially abolished in New York, but even when legally freed, black people faced many difficulties. Some of the black population formed a new middle class and some, facing discrimination, remained in poverty.

CONTROLLING IMMIGRATION

For most immigrants, New York offered hope of a new life. They were brought over for labour on the huge construction works that were taken place, but were held in suspicion and for society's ills. New Yorkers soon started trying to control the flow of new arrivals. A "sorting office" was first established at Castle Garden, and then **Ellis Island**; 20 000 immigrants passed through here each day, including 16 million Europeans, before it closed in 1924. Many of them were heading to the west of the country, but a good deal settled in New York, causing a sensational rise in population, from 500 000 inhabitants in 1850 to more than 3 million in 1900, making it the most populated city in the world. New York became an emblem of liberty, and Jewish people fleeing persecution were joined by Italian immigrants, and then Chinese people. Rich immigrants had no difficulty getting established in the city, but most of these new arrivals were plunged into a most precarious existence. Communities tended to group together in the same areas (Little Italy, Chinatown, Lower East Side), giving the city its defining diverse identity.

Cosmopolitan New York

A MULTIETHNIC CITY

New York is the most ethnically diverse city in the United States. Walking through the streets you'll hear a cornucopia of languages, especially Spanish, Mandarin and Cantonese. Its wealth of diversity is evident in the huge variety of food served, from burgers to Jamaican curry, Tibetan dumplings to duck confit. The city has more than 8.6 million inhabitants. Almost 37% are foreign born, and nearly 50% speak non-English languages at home. The highest contingent of immigrants today come from the Dominican Republic, China, Jamaica, Guyana and Mexico, though there are also arrivals from Bangladesh, Nigeria, Ghana, the Philippines, Russia and Ukraine.

COMMUNITIES

One of the characteristics of New York is the strong presence of distinct communities. Many visitors are surprised by the specificity of the pockets of the city. Sometimes you just need to cross the road to pass into another continent. The historic communities have often made their areas famous: Jewish people in the Lower East Side, Upper West Side and Williamsburg, Italians in Little Italy (Manhattan) and in the Bronx,

and Poles in Greenpoint. Sometimes communities can be found in unexpected places; for example, there are still many people from China in Manhattan's Chinatown, but the area has now been overtaken by Flushing, Queens. Then there are cultural enclaves spread throughout the city, such as Ukrainian "Little Odessa" in Brighton Beach; Koreatown along 32nd Street in Manhattan; the Caribbean areas around Flatbush Avenue in Brooklyn; Dominicans in the Bronx; Senegalese people on 116th Street, between Nicholas and 8th Avenues; a Turkish community, also in Brighton Beach; Brazilians and Greeks in Astoria, Queens, and Indians in Jackson Heights, Queens.

A COSMOPOLITAN CUISINE

There is no single kind of New York cuisine: you'll find everything. If it exists in the world, you'll probably find it in New York. The 20,000-plus restaurants of the city offer classic American fare but also Italian, Jewish, Ukrainian, Korean, Indian, Bangladeshi, Chinese, Cuban, Nigerian, Colombian, South African, Australian and more. The different influences mix too, creating new kinds of cuisine. Some particularly New York foods, like bagels and pizza, will always be staples.

Economy and Finance

New York owes its rapid development to the exceptional position of its port and the opening of the Erie Canal. Today the port activity is contained to just a few piers.

REAL ESTATE AND INDUSTRY

The building sector has always enjoyed success. In the 1950s and '60s, slums were demolished and large housing complexes were created in their place, while public highways were developed and the bridges and subway lines updated. In the next few decades, the focus would be on preserving the older heritage of the city. Speculation was centered around abandoned industrial sites and ports located beyond the East River. The cost of rent and the competition caused by globalization forced industries out, and jobs fell by half from 1950. Dressmaking and tailoring continued in the Garment District, but the kind of work was now limited to only high-end items. The high education level of the inhabitants of the city and its immigrants favored the development of technology, as well as the medical sector and computing. Food, high-end mechanics and the chemical industries also held up.

PRESS AND ENTERTAINMENT

New York is a bastion of the press, synonymous with independent thinking. The city is the home of no less than 15 newspapers and nearly 300 magazines, as well as press and photo agencies, national television channels and a good number of cable TV channels. The city, where bibliophiles have always been in abundance, is also home to major publishing houses. Countless congresses and conventions are held here. A significant entertainment industry has also developed over the years with the many concert halls, theaters and cabarets. New York is also, of course, the site of some of the most famous museums on the planet.

WALL STREET AND FINANCE

The **New York Stock Exchange** (NYSE), aka Wall Street, is the definitive symbol of capitalism and the world's most important stock market. Brokers trade values of $42bn. every day. A substantial proportion of international finance passes through the hands of these brokers amounting to huge sums, which, in turn act as a waterfall, irrigating the economic networks of New York, in particular the professions attached to finance. These jobs create and maintain in turn a myriad of services at every level of city life.
The world of finance was however severely shaken by the crisis of 2008, which created a new push for the regulation of financial activity.

Design and Architecture

SEARCHING FOR A STYLE

The English turned New York into a North American trading post on the foundations of a Dutch city; along the muddy roads, Georgian-style houses were built with curved eaves, colonnades and pediments.

After their victory over the English, the settlers were inspired by the architecture of the Roman Republic. The **Federal style** was characterized by symmetrical and square constructions, with classical ornamentation, columns sometimes raised on pediments and imposts, as well as the use of elliptical windows. The mayor DeWitt Clinton (1769-1828) was responsible for the planning of the road grid, with avenues laid out at right angles. The Randel Plan, the famous "grid" of Manhattan, with its 2028 blocks, was thus created in 1811. The **neo-Grec style** was all the rage from 1820, characterized by marble and large pediments framed with Doric, Ionic and Corinthian style colonnades (Federal Hall). Churches and whole roads (Cushman Row) were constructed in relativity austere style. But as it was enjoying economic boom, the city was ravaged by a huge fire (1835). The **neo-Gothic style** came next. It plays on asymmetry, the picturesque, the profusion of turrets, niches, and long, narrow oblong-shaped windows. It became the fashion for new mansions, with an emphasis on finely worked gables, spires and gargoyles. A want for excess born of the end of the Victorian era lead to **Queen Anne style**, where yet more ornamentation was added (1880-1905). With a combination of influences mixing Byzantine and medieval, the **neo-Romanesque** style emerged. It was characterized by massive towers and heavy semi-circular arches in cut stone, as well as bas-reliefs, and cast iron gate copies.

INFLUENCES AND ECLECTICISM

As Romantic and Gothic trends developed, architects turned towards Italy and Paris for inspiration. The **Italian style** (1840-1880) also benefited from the use of cast iron in architecture with its rectangular appearance, raised front steps and finely arched narrow windows. In the south part of Manhattan, the use of cast iron allowed for the construction of higher buildings, leading to the creation of the first skyscrapers. Architects and developers would experiment with the assembly of prefabricated iron pieces, slotted with glistening glass once in situ. Houses were often coated in inexpensive chocolate-colored sandstone, giving them their name, "brownstones". By extension the same term would also be applied to the houses of the same areas, built in brick or other kinds of stone.

The French **Second Empire style** (1860-1880) would also influence New York, with zinc rooftops and mansard-style top floors becoming popular. This style was followed by a vogue for **neoclassical and Beaux-Arts**, inspired by Paris, with grand structures featuring arcades and monumental entrances embellished by columns and statues (see main branch of New York Public Library).

CONQUERING THE SKIES

The real revolution would come not so much from changing styles, bur rather the aim to build high into the sky. If the initial motivation was speculative — to fit in the most construction possible in the smallest space available — it was this decision to build ever-higher that changed the look of the city most definitively. In 1857, Elisha Otis invented the elevator. The American Institute of Architects was created in New York in the same year. A little later, a particularly innovative school opened in Chicago, where the first skyscraper would be built. In New York, the **Flatiron Building** (1902) was the first of a series of buildings that would constitute the famous Manhattan skyline. Skyscrapers sprouted up like mushrooms throughout the 20C. A new European fashion, **Art Nouveau**, came over, followed in 1925 by **Art Deco**. The latter was characterized by recesses, playing with vertical harmonies, buildings coated in stone and varnished brick or metal (see Chrysler Building,

Empire State Building). After the Second World War, in reaction to the luxurious tastes of the time, buildings were constructed in **"international" style**, with clean lines, rectilinear layouts and glass walls and surfaces (see UN headquarters, MoMA). The last two decades of the 20C, called **postmodern**, saw the use of features such as iridescent colored glasswork, and stone made a marked comeback in the paving of esplanades and atria (see World Financial Center, World Trade Center, Guggenheim Museum, Whitney Museum).

THE 21ST CENTURY

The collapse of the World Trade Center in 2001, marked a turning point for the city. As well as the symbolic construction of 1 World Trade Center, the whole horizon of New York was also redesigned. The successive closure of the major port spaces left huge virgin terrains, prime for development. The riverbanks of Brooklyn and Queens, with a view over the towers of Midtown, quickly began housing a number of new projects, while in Manhattan towers would shoot up, designed by famous names such as Jean Nouvel, Zaha Hadid and Herzog & de Meuron. Perhaps most significantly, the monumental Hudson Yards began. To accomodate the expansion of the city, a new subway line on 2nd Avenue began opening, and an extension of line 7 was also built.

Flatiron Building

Modern Art

Until the start of the 20C, American painting was inwards-looking, turning towards nature or society.

THE EIGHT

It was in February 1908 that a thunderbolt would amplify the impressionist revolution in America. Seven young painters, brought together around **Robert Henry**, would exhibit at the Macbeth Gallery. They painted the smoke and the grime of the city, the exhaustion of the workers, and lust, and proved that there was beauty to be found in sweat and tears. This earned them the nickname **Ashcan School** (from ash can). This movement was followed by a period of artistic tumult, which would reach its zenith at the Exhibition of Independent Artists (1910) and especially at the Armory Show (1913), the largest art exhibition ever held in the United States.

THE AMERICAN AVANT-GARDE

Marcel Duchamp presented his *Nude Descending a Staircase* in the US which would create a public scandal, but would help his fellow painters in their experiments. In a few short but crucial years, the gallery of Alfred Stieglitz on 5th Avenue would exhibit **Georgia O'Keeffe** and **Arthur Dove**, the first American abstract artist, as well as **Charles Demuth** and **Charles Sheeler**, specialists in urban hyperrealism

THE GREAT FIGURES

New York was suddenly cast into the spotlight by the work of **Edward Hopper**, whose art was a remarkable meditation on modern American life. During the Great Depression, **Thomas Benton**, **Grant Wood**, **Reginald Marsh**, **Ben Shahn** and **John Curry** would examine the American way of life. In 1936, Mark Rothko, Arshile Gorky, Willem De Kooning, Robert Motherwell and Jackson Pollock would form the core of the **American Abstract Artists** (AAA). They constituted, after 1945, the first school of painting with international reach; abstract expressionism was also known as the "New York School". With the addition of famous artists forced to flee across the Atlantic during the War, such as **Léger**, **Miró** and **Ernst**, they would turn the artistic landscape on its head. In 1958, **Leo Castelli** opened in the Upper East Side his reputation-making gallery (Castelli Gallery). A new generation of artists was born. **Andy Warhol** and pop art would change the face of contemporary art, which would move into the streets. New York now had a strong place in the art market; public spaces would welcome work by Dubuffet, Tony Rosenthal, Henry Moore, Jim Dine, Fritz Koenig and Milton Hebald.

The Legend of Broadway

In the **Theater District**, there are around 40 venues with 500 seats, of which more than two thirds show only musicals; this ensemble constitutes the official Broadway, or "on Broadway". Hugely successful and popular shows run in these theaters. Below 500 seats, venues are called "off Broadway" and welcome young and starting actors. For actors, performing on Broadway is synonymous with recognition.

THE THEATER

Eugene O'Neill (1888-1953), born in New York, is the most famous North American playwright. Throughout his career, he would explore the darkest aspects of the human condition, with his plays exploring a world of marginalized people and despair. **John Steinbeck** (*Of Mice and Men*, 1937), is highly acclaimed by many for his works. **Arthur Miller** (1915-2005) wrote short-form plays, such as *Death of a Salesman* (1949) and *The Crucible* (1953). Among more contemporary writers, **Sam Shepard**, writer, screenwriter and actor, is also a well-regarded playwright, from the writing of his sketches for theatrical revue *O! Calcutta*. **August Wilson** (1945-2005), two-time winner of the Pulitzer Prize for *Fences* and *The Piano Lesson*, was a great Afro-American writer, describing through a series of ten plays (*The Pittsburgh Cycle*), aspects of the African-American experience over a period of 100 years. **Wendy Wasserstein** (1950-2006), born in Brooklyn, was another major playwright and winner of the Pulitzer Prize for Drama for *The Heidi Chronicles* (1989).

MUSICAL THEATER

The section of Broadway in line with Times Square has become a place of legend. The first musical, *The Black Crook,* played to sold-out crowds in 1866. Encouraged by its success, producers would develop this genre. In the 1920s and '30s, one musical followed another and their songs became huge hits. **Fred Astaire** and **Gene Kelly** danced on to people's cinema screens. Musicals reached a zenith in 1957, Stephen Sondheim's *West Side Story*, with music composed by Leonard Bernstein, made its premiere at the Winter Garden. The legend of Romeo and Juliet was transposed onto the working-class areas of 1950s New York, creating a sensational success. For some years now, many musicals have been inspired by the films of Walt Disney, such as *The Lion King* and *Mary Poppins,* but also more varied themes, such as the legendary *Les Misérables,* adapted from a novel by Victor Hugo. *Cats* has been performed more than 9000 times since its creation in 1981. Today, *The Book of Mormon* and *Hamilton* are among some of the shows taking center stage.

Andy Warhol and Pop Art

POP ART

Roy Lichtenstein, **Robert Rauschenberg**, **Jasper Johns** and especially Andy Warhol and the ultra-cool coterie that frequented his Factory were the principal players of pop art, the motor of a frenetic speculative machine that made New York the world capital of the art market. Drawing inspiration from the ad houses for which they worked, from comic strips and the current affairs of their time, Andy Warhol and Roy Lichtenstein made everyday life the subject of their art. Their totally innovative and easy-to-reproduce art centered around real-life objects and they approached their subjects mechanically, using repetition and mixing colors to create a subtle harmony.

ANDY WARHOL (1928-1987)

He started out drawing advertisements for magazines and looking after the displays of a department store. He very quickly carried out his first canvasses, taking inspiration from comic strips. His bottles of Coca-Cola and Campbell's soup cans were a dramatic success. He moved into silkscreen printing, which would allow him to reproduce his subjects as many times as he liked. He won recognition immediately. A loft, the Factory, was his workshop.

A multitude of collaborators helped him to create his ideas from his sketches. Cold, cynical and intelligent, he was held in adulation by the New York jet-set, as well as regular New-Yorkers who identified with the themes his work explored. He undertook a series of now-iconic, portraits: Marilyn Monroe, Elvis Presley, Jackie Kennedy, Mao Zedong and Lenin, as well as Mona Lisa and huge multicolored repeated flower prints. Passionate about the tools of cinematography, he directed a number of art films featuring improvising characters.

AFTER POP ART

The wild spike in prices and the unequal nature and quality of exhibitions formed a bubble that would suck in investors. Art became snobbish and it would be felt in the quality of the work. From this profusion of work, occasionally a pearl would emerge, such as **Jean-Michel Basquiat** (1960-1988) whose raging and hallucinatory genius, synthesized different cultural references and pop art, with the style he developed as a street artist and tagger in New York. At this time, many working-class areas (Harlem, Bronx, Queens) were covered in murals, becoming ephemeral open-air galleries.

Mural by Nychos the Weird in Bushwick, Brooklyn

Literature

Writers who were born or lived in New York, such as Herman Melville, were not always inspired by their own city. From the 19C onwards, however **Washington Irving** wrote *A History of New York* (1809), **Stephen Crane** caused a scandal with New York street slang in *Maggie: A Girl of the Streets* (1893); **Edith Wharton** (1862-1937) offered superb descriptions of New York high society in *The House of Mirth* (1905) and *The Age of Innocence* (1920). **F. Scott Fitzgerald** described the New York of the Roaring Twenties and the corruption of the American dream in *The Great Gatsby* (1925).

MANHATTAN: CITY OF THE THRILLER

With *Manhattan Transfer* (1925) by **John Dos Passos**, the New York literature of the 20C was born, as was the case in Europe with *Ulysses* by James Joyce and *Journey to the End of the Night* by Céline. *Manhattan Transfer* is a comprehensive work, run through with jazz rhythms and the explosion of Cubist painting. New York appears like a well-oiled machine where chaos reigns. A kind of literature tried to make sense of this disorder: the noir novel and the thriller. *City of the Dead* by Herbert Lieberman (1991), *The Alienist* by Caleb Carr (1995) and *Bone* by George Chesbro (1993) would give back some faith in humanity. **Dashiell Hammett**, creator of the great Sam Spade, one of literature's most iconic private detectives (*The Maltese Falcon*, 1929), described like no other the corruption of the city in a distinctive pared-down style. **Chester Himes** with *The Five Cornered Square* (1958) would inaugurate the Harlem patrols of black cops Coffin Ed Johnson and Gravedigger Jones.

BEYOND GENRES

Writers and poets would naturally begin to meet to exchange ideas. **Greenwich Village** welcomed Mark Twain, Henry James, Melville and the playwright Eugene O'Neill, the poet Edna St Vincent Millay, Theodore Dreiser and Thomas Wolfe. Dylan Thomas was followed by the **Beat Generation**, defined by names such as William Burroughs, Allen Ginsberg and Jack Kerouac. The most famous of these circles would be the **Algonquin Round Table**, named after a hotel bar, where the members of prestigious *The New Yorker* would make and unmake reputations. Public readings were held amid the cultural circle and literary prizes, like the **Pulitzer** and the **National Book Award**, were awarded. Some writers would keep their distance from the media such as J.D. Salinger (1951-2010), author of *The Catcher in the Rye*.

Among famous literary New-Yorkers are Tom Wolfe, Truman Capote, Joan Didion, Nora Ephron, Grace Paley, Toni Morrison, Hubert Selby Jr., Jay McInerney and Paul Auster.

Filming New York

In the beginnings of the film industry, the Eastman-Edison trust would shoot its films in greater New York. But in 1908, its competitors left for Hollywood, where prices were lower and space more readily available. New York remained a photogenic site, appreciated by directors and would still be the backdrop of various films and televised series.

CINEMA INDUSTRY

Despite the attraction of Hollywood, independent filmmakers chose to work in New York: John Cassavetes, Abel Ferrara, Amos Kollek, Jim Jarmusch, Spike Lee, Martin Scorsese and Woody Allen, who made an icon of Manhattan in his films.
The creation in 1947 of the Actors Studio in New York marked a turning point in the history of New York cinema. It would train a whole host of stars, including Marlon Brando, James Dean and Robert De Niro, a favorite of Martin Scorsese. The city houses some of the best film schools—the Tisch School of the Arts at NYU, the School of Visual Arts, the New School and the film departments of Columbia University—as well as the **American Museum of the Moving Image** (&. *p. 100*). Distribution has also progressed a great deal. Well-equipped cinema spaces have blossomed and festivals attract enthusiasts : **Tribeca Film Festival**, run by De Niro (April), Human Rights Watch Film Festival (June), Dance

on Camera Festival (July), New York Film Festival (Oct) NewFest : New York LGBT Film Festival (Oct), Williamsburg Independent Film Festival (Nov).

FROM CINEMA TO TELEVISION

The renaissance of New York's film studios owes a lot to television, and it's now very uncommon to see filming around the city. Cult series such as *Sex and the City*, *The Sopranos*, *Gossip Girl* and *NYPD* were known to huge audiences and many still make pilgrimages to filming locations featured in them. As well as series, the entertainment show *Saturday Night Live,* broadcast live every Saturday night, is another televisual event. It launched stars including Bill Murray, Kristen Wiig and Tina Fey.

LEGENDARY SITES

The cinema of New York has created some powerful images over the years, such as King Kong climbing the **Empire State Building**. Hitchcock showed Cary Grant attempting to escape his pursuers at the **Plaza Hotel** (*North by Northwest*, 1959); you may also remember Dustin Hoffman running around **Central Park** reservoir (*Marathon Man*, 1976). A more romantic atmosphere floats around Woody Allen and Diane Keaton in front of the fountain in Bryant Park in *Manhattan* (1979).

Music

CLASSICAL MUSIC

As well as the Metropolitan Opera House, the city offers Carnegie Hall and Lincoln Center. The biggest soloists and opera singers regularly perform the works of renowned composers such as Dvořák and Tchaikovsky.

THE SYMBOL OF AMERICA

Though jazz originated in New Orleans at the end of the 19C, New York welcomed its greatest creators. Jazz and dance clubs blossomed in the 1920s in Harlem. The Cotton Club, on Lenox Avenue, received **Duke Ellington**, **Count Basie** and **Cab Calloway**. In 1924, **George Gershwin** performed his jazz-style piece *Rhapsody in Blue*. Later, a number of significant clubs could be found on 52nd Street, without it dethroning Harlem; this was where **Ella Fitzgerald** triumphed in 1935. **Gospel** shook the churches of New York with its rousing rhythms. Lester Young and Coleman Hawkins enjoyed the heyday of the **swing** period in New York. From 1945-1948, the **bebop revolution**, animated by **Dizzy Gillespie** and **Charlie Parker** unfolded throughout the city. Modern jazz would be built on its foundations, characterized by geniuses such as **Thelonious Monk**, **John Coltrane** and **Miles Davis**. New York is also

where the devotees of **free jazz** were recruited in the 1960s and 70s, before the advent of the contemporary period of jazz. Today, all the genre's iterations can be found in New York, from the most conventional at Lincoln Center to trendy clubs and open-air summer festivals.

ROCK, FOLK, PUNK, RAP

If the **Velvet Underground** were the standard bearers, some New York rock groups also could or can rival their British counterparts; talents span a range of styles (Ramones, New York Dolls, Sonic Youth, The Strokes, Pavement, Interpol and more recently MGMT and Vampire Weekend). **Patti Smith** and **Lou Reed** brought a poetic touch to the starker sound of the scene, and quality recording studios often attract top artists. The city itself also inspires artists such as Norah Jones, Bob Dylan, U2 and Simon & Garfunkel, who celebrate it in their songs. *New York, New York* (sung by Frank Sinatra) is perhaps the most famous song about the city. New York is also the city of rappers and **hip-hop** (Jay-Z, Nas, Mase, Public Enemy) who tell the story of New York street life, chiming culturally with street art. Today you'll often see music performances in the streets and subway stations of New York.

Saxophonist in front of Carnegie Hall
© H. Matsumoto/The Image Bank/Getty Images

Maps

Inside

Cover

Photo credits

Page 4

Greenwich Village: © Directphoto/age fotostock
Central Park: © Kathia Tamanaha/iStock
Museum of Modern Art: © 2019 The Museum of Modern Art. Photo: Jonathan Muzikar
One World Observatory: © Alex Spatari/Moment Open/Getty Images
Metropolitan Museum of Art: © S. Reboredo/age fotostock

Page 5

Empire State Building: © M. Colombo/Moment/Getty Images
Brooklyn Bridge: © kasto80/iStock
Times Square: © Mlenny/iStock
Soho: © Jose Peral/age fotostock
Statue of Liberty: © ozgurdonmaz/iStock

THEGREENGUIDE short-stays **New York**

Editorial Director	Cynthia Ochterbeck
Editor	Sophie Friedman
Translator	Hannah Meltzer
Contributing Writer	Becky Cheang
Production Manager	Natasha George
Cartography	Peter Wrenn, Nicolas Breton
Picture Editor	Yoshimi Kanazawa
Interior Design	Laurent Muller
Layout	Natasha George

Contact Us

Michelin Travel and Lifestyle North America
One Parkway South
Greenville, SC 29615
USA
travel.lifestyle@us.michelin.com

Michelin Travel Partner
Hannay House
39 Clarendon Road
Watford, Herts WD17 1JA
UK
✆01923 205240
travelpubsales@uk.michelin.com
www.viamichelin.co.uk

Special Sales

For information regarding bulk sales,
customized editions and premium sales,
please contact us at:
travel.lifestyle@us.michelin.com

YOUR OPINION IS ESSENTIAL
TO IMPROVING OUR PRODUCTS

*Help us by answering the
questionnaire on our website:*
satisfaction.michelin.com

Michelin Travel Partner

Société par actions simplifiées au capital de 15 044 940 EUR
27 cours de l'Ile Seguin - 92100 Boulogne Billancourt (France)
R.C.S. Nanterre 433 677 721

© Michelin Travel Partner
ISBN 978-2-067243-16-3
Printed: March 2020
Printer: ESTIMPRIM